THE
MASS

THE
MASS

The Glory, the Mystery, the Tradition

Cardinal Donald Wuerl
and Mike Aquilina

Foreword by ARCHBISHOP J. AUGUSTINE DI NOIA, O.P.,
*Secretary of the Congregation for Divine Worship
and the Discipline of the Sacraments*

Preface by CARDINAL FRANCIS GEORGE,
Archbishop of Chicago

DOUBLEDAY
NEW YORK   LONDON   TORONTO   SYDNEY   AUCKLAND

ꓒꓒ
DOUBLEDAY

Published in the United States by Doubleday Religion,
an imprint of the Crown Publishing Group, a division of
Random House, Inc., New York.
www.crownpublishing.com
www.doubledayreligion.com

DOUBLEDAY and the DD colophon are registered trademarks of
Random House, Inc.

Library of Congress Cataloging-in-Publication Data is available upon request.

ISBN 978-0-307-71880-8

PRINTED IN THE UNITED STATES OF AMERICA

Book design by Ellen Cipriano
Jacket photograph: Michael Hoyt

1   3   5   7   9   10   8   6   4   2

First Edition

CONTENTS

A Note from the Authors

Before we began writing this book together, we had known each other for many years. We have prayed together, worked together, and shared the same Eucharistic table— but with a difference. One of us approached the altar as a priest-celebrant; the other as a lay Catholic, husband, and father. In the pages of this book, we try to present both of those perspectives on the Mass, so that readers might experience a "panoramic" view of the central act of Christian worship—an action instituted by Jesus Christ and entrusted to his Church.

We took to writing this book because we share an ardent love for the Mass. We have written much about the Mass down through the years, and spoken often on the subject, and some of that material has found its way into these pages.

For both of us, the Mass is the foundation and center of every day's activity. We want to encourage that same appreciation in those in the Church, in the neighborhood, and in the home who share our faith.

The book arose, then, out of our common interest and common devotion, and our desire to make that interest and devotion much more common than it is today. When we say "common," however, we don't mean "low" or "pedestrian." We mean "ordinary." We pray that this book might in some small way help readers to make the Mass a more regular and even necessary part of their days. We hope they, in turn, will share their renewed fervor with others.

Our immediate occasion for taking on such a large project was the approval by the United States bishops, in collaboration with the English-speaking bishops around the world, of a new translation of the Roman Missal. We believe this is a key part of the New Evangelization called for by our Holy Father, Pope Benedict XVI. He used the word "re-propose" to describe the New Evangelization. We need to re-propose our belief in Christ and his Gospel for the sake of those who are convinced that they "already know" the faith and that it offers nothing interesting. We want to invite them to hear it all over again, as if for the first time.

We pray that our book will be useful to believers as they speak and hear new words of worship and praise, in a rite that is, like the Gospel, ever ancient and ever new.

Cardinal Donald Wuerl

Mike Aquilina

Foreword

By Archbishop J. Augustine Di Noia, O.P.,
Secretary of the Congregation for Divine Worship and
the Discipline of the Sacraments

The authors begin this book with a phrase that is simple and seemingly self-evident: "The Mass is what Catholics do." By frequently citing the earliest Christian witnesses—the Scriptures and the Church fathers—the authors go on to demonstrate that the Mass is what Catholics have always done.

The Mass is present always and everywhere. It's simply what Catholics do, as long as we have life's breath. Indeed, we can say that it's like breathing. It keeps us spiritually alive. It's a sign that we are still living the life God has given us, in the way God has made us to live it.

Breathing is constant, commonplace. We breathe without thinking about it—unless it's impeded for some reason. It's simply what we do. Yet biologists tell us it is anything but simple. Every breath is a rich and complex event that affects all our bodily systems, right down to our constituent chemistry.

The Mass, too, is constant and commonplace. Yet it is also rich and complex. Every word and gesture has a history, a significance, a meaning.

This is the way God makes things. Even the simplest and most elemental events signify processes that are vital, essential, and beautiful, if examined.

What is commonplace we tend to treat as unimportant. We treat such events the way we do respiration, as something done unthinkingly. We go through the motions.

We must not allow this to happen to the Mass. Yet too often we do. Thus, as long as the Church has celebrated the Mass, its teachers have done what the authors of this book have done. They have explained or unveiled the signs and mysteries of the Mass. The fathers of the ancient Church even had a word for this type of preaching. They called it, in Greek, *mystagogia*—guidance through the mysteries. It is also called "liturgical catechesis." Its aim, according to the Church's Catechism, is "to initiate people into the mystery of Christ . . . by proceeding from the visible to the invisible, from the sign to the thing signified, from the 'sacraments' to the 'mysteries' " (Catechism of the Catholic Church [CCC] n. 1075).

We find this "mystagogical" approach best exemplified in the works of the giants of the early Church: Saint Cyril of Jerusalem, Saint Ambrose of Milan, Saint John Chrysostom, and Saint Augustine. We find it in the New Testament as well, in Saint John's Gospel, in the Letter to the Hebrews, and in the First Letter of Saint Peter.

As long as the sacraments have been "what Catholics do," the Church's teachers have taught about the sacraments in this way.

In the year 2007 Pope Benedict XVI called for a renewal of such teaching. He was himself responding to the requests of a synod of bishops that had gathered in Rome to discuss the Eucharist. (The cardinal-coauthor of this book was an active participant in that synod.) The synod fathers "asked that the faithful be helped to make their interior dispositions correspond to their gestures and words." Otherwise, the Holy Father indicated, they could risk falling into "ritualism," which is really a sort of superstition. He called for "an education in Eucharistic faith capable of enabling the faithful to live personally what they celebrate."

This book is an answer to that call. It is unusual because it is truly a collaboration between a prelate and a layman—two men who have experienced the Mass daily, for decades, but from different sides of the sanctuary. Thus the authors are able to present the view from the pew and the view from the altar, and to draw them together as the view of the whole Church, both laity and clergy. Cardinal Wuerl and Mike Aquilina are able to articulate the questions that arise in the minds of worshippers, and answer them in an engaging and accurate way. They follow closely the method Pope Benedict outlined for mystagogical teaching in his apostolic exhortation *Sacramentum Caritatis.* The Holy Father's outline is worth quoting at length:

  a. *It interprets the rites in the light of the events of our salvation,* in accordance with the Church's living tradition. The celebration of the Eucharist, in its infinite richness, makes constant reference to salvation history. In Christ crucified and risen, we truly celebrate the one who has united all things in himself (cf. Ephesians 1:10). From the beginning, the Christian community has interpreted the events of Jesus' life, and the Paschal Mystery in particular, in relation to the entire history of the Old Testament.

b. A mystagogical catechesis must also be concerned with *presenting the meaning of the signs* contained in the rites. This is particularly important in a highly technological age like our own, which risks losing the ability to appreciate signs and symbols. More than simply conveying information, a mystagogical catechesis should be capable of making the faithful more sensitive to the language of signs and gestures which, together with the word, make up the rite.

c. Finally, a mystagogical catechesis must be concerned with bringing out the *significance of the rites for the Christian life* in all its dimensions— work and responsibility, thoughts and emotions, activity and repose. Part of the mystagogical process is to demonstrate how the mysteries celebrated in the rite are linked to the missionary responsibility of the faithful. The mature fruit of mystagogy is an awareness that one's life is being progressively transformed by the holy mysteries being celebrated. The aim of all Christian education, moreover, is to train the believer in an adult faith that can make him a "new creation," capable of bearing witness in his surroundings to the Christian hope that inspires him.

The Holy Father expresses his hope that this work of education would extend to the "whole people of God," and so we may hope that this book will find a wide audience.

Such an audience would indeed be capable of full, conscious, and active participation in the Mass. The measure of mystagogy's effectiveness, according to Pope Benedict, is a congregation's reverence—"an increased sense of the mystery of God present among us."

This is the mystery contained in the signs of the Mass. God is present as he promised he would be. This is the mystery of an event more significant, and more life-giving, than the breaths we take.

Preface

*By Cardinal Francis George,
Archbishop of Chicago*

When we speak of the Mass, we cannot help but confront profound mysteries. This is as true today as it was in the first days of the Church. Saint Paul looked to the Mass as the sign of Christian unity, but also the source of Christian unity: "Because the loaf of bread is one, we, though many, are one body, for we all partake of the one loaf" (1 Corinthians 10:17). The Mass makes the Church even as the Church, empowered by Christ, makes the Mass.

This is a great mystery. Yet it is only one aspect of the Mass. If we ponder the doctrine, if we pray for light, we will discover that the Mass has many dimensions. It is Christ's sacrifice on Calvary, now made present in an unbloody manner in the sacrament of the altar. It is a banquet where we are fed by the living Christ and come to deep and intimate union with him. It is Christ's real presence, a unique presence, a presence not just in action, but in himself: body and blood, soul and divinity. Our Eucharist is a "who," not a "what." It is Someone.

If we profess the Catholic faith, there should be nothing more important to us than active participation in this mystery. And that's the goal of every page of this book. Through words and pictures, the authors help us grow in our knowledge and understanding of the Mass, its whole and its parts, its essence and even its furnishings. The authors have undertaken an important task. They have provided a needed service.

For active participation in the Mass is the very soul of participation in the life of the Church. The Church exists first of all to worship God, and to worship him as he wants to be worshipped. Our worship of the Father is possible because we are "in Christ" through baptism and faith. By actively participating in the liturgy, we open ourselves to the mystery. We cooperate personally with Christ in all he seeks to do for us and through us. In the celebration of the Mass, Jesus Christ is the one who acts as both priest and victim, the one offering and the one being offered or sacrificed. To his self-sacrifice, we join our own, our very selves.

There is a certain *objectivity* about the Mass because it begins with Christ, not with our religious experience. The Mass is the action of Christ himself, made visible and shared through the sacramental action of the Church. Its basic symbol system comes to us from the apostles, and the Church is not free to change it. If someone "consecrates" corn bread or chocolate cake rather than bread made from wheat, there is no sacramental action; no Mass is celebrated. The sacramental signs make visible the action of the risen Lord, and the

Church is not free to change them. Since religion is a purely personal project for many people today, this recognition of limits can be confounding. But those who argue about the essentials of the sacraments are arguing with Christ, not with the Church.

If we accept Christ on his own terms, our time is better spent trying to understand the symbols he gave us, rather than attempting to reject or replace them. Our time is better spent with this book, by Cardinal Donald Wuerl and Mike Aquilina.

There is also, however, a "subjectivity" about the Mass, because Christ calls us to cooperate with him in his actions. We participate in something only the Lord can accomplish; we take part in his action in order to become "one body, one spirit in Christ." In the liturgy we are brought into contact with the saving work of Christ made present under the sacramental signs. There, God's grace transforms us into Christ's own likeness. Our response to Christ's action, the kernel of our active participation in the liturgy, is twofold: we adore and we obey. In and through adoration, we respond to the infinite God who is our creator and redeemer. Through obedience, we accept and allow the God whom we adore to shape our personal existence in the pattern of his love.

The Mass involves us with Christ's action in union with all those who are his disciples, living and dead. Sacred art often depicts the saints who have gone before us in faith and whose feasts are marked in the liturgical calendar. Church art gives us beautiful crucifixes, splendidly crafted chalices, and other objects needed for worship. Music lifts our voices

and our hearts to God. Christ's actions are made present in
the sacramental rites; our faith is made visible in the art and
music and architecture that surround them.

Again, however, the experience is richer if we approach
it with greater understanding—which, again, this book prepares us to do.

It arrives at an opportune moment, as the bishops of the
English-speaking world are about to publish a new translation of the latest edition of the Roman Missal. The Missal
was revised after the Second Vatican Council (1962–1965)
and published under the authority of Pope Paul VI. Since
the late 1960s, the Holy See has published three subsequent
editions of the post–Vatican II Missal. With the appearance
of the most recent edition, the U.S. bishops decided the time
was right for a fresh English translation. The new texts, now
just beginning to reach our parishes, are both beautiful and
interesting. Still, they are superseding prayers that have been
familiar to Catholics for an entire generation. The transition
will take some time and certainly require effort of those
who want to pray them well and with understanding.

You have begun well if you have begun with this book.

THE
MASS

Introduction:
The Mass Is What We Do

THE MASS IS WHAT CATHOLICS DO. It's the heart of Catholic life, for individuals and for the community.

A Catholic may fill up hours with devotional prayers and volunteer service, public witness and almsgiving. A parish may sponsor a school and a soup kitchen, a scouting troop and several Bible study groups.

The Mass, however, is the heart that gives life to all of it. Our tradition describes the Mass beautifully as "the source and summit of the whole Christian life." Catholicism means many things to the world. It has inspired the art and architecture of the great masters. Our sanctuaries have echoed with masterworks of music. Our saints have served the poorest of the poor. Yet all these things we trace back to a single source: the Mass.

Catholics think of the Mass as synonymous with the parish church. Whether we say "I went to church" or "I went to Mass," we mean the same thing. Even if we do many other things at our church, the Mass is what the building was made for. To "go to church" is to go to Mass. This is true for every Catholic. When the pope travels to distant lands, the news media pay close attention—and the world watches as he simply does what Catholics do: he celebrates Mass, sometimes for a congregation of hundreds of thousands of people.

Yet such a large-scale event is no greater than the usual Mass in an ordinary parish. It is the same, in its essence, as a Mass that a military chaplain offers on the hood of a Jeep during a lull in a battle.

The Mass is the most familiar and recognizable element of the Catholic faith; and still it is also the most enigmatic. In the Mass we see postures, gestures, and items of clothing that would seem out of place anywhere else. We hear words that hint at deep and ancient mysteries. Even the more fa-

Two deacons lead Pope Benedict XVI at the start of a Mass celebrated for nearly fifty thousand people at Nationals Park in Washington, D.C., on April 17, 2008. © *Catholic News Service*/L'Osservatore Romano *via Reuters*

miliar words sometimes mean something quite different from their meaning in ordinary usage.

The words, the vestments, and the gestures of the Mass took their origins in times long past. Nevertheless, they hold infinite meaning for Catholics today. For we believe that the Son of God took flesh and became man in a particular time and place, and that he used the language and culture of that time and place to convey truths that speak to every age and nation. Jesus insisted on this point; and so, "on the night he was handed over, took bread, and after he had given thanks, broke it and said, 'This is my body that is for you. Do this in remembrance of me.' In the same way also the cup, after supper, saying, 'This cup is the new covenant in my blood. Do this, as often as you drink it, in remembrance of me.' For as often as you eat this bread and drink the cup, you proclaim the death of the Lord until he comes" (1 Corinthians 11:23–26).

He said, "Do this," and so *this*—the Mass—is what we Catholics do.

We find the experience more rewarding, however, when we understand the Mass as we pray it. And that's the reason for this book.

In the chapters that follow, we'll look at all the elements that go together to make up a typical Mass. We'll define some basic terms. We'll outline the parts of the ritual. We'll look at each and every part from up close. We'll examine the prayers. We'll discuss the vessels and the vestments used in the ritual. We'll speak a bit about doctrine. We'll trace some prayers and practices back to their historical and biblical roots. We'll take a slow walk through the Mass, stopping to see the sights along the way.

It's not a very original idea, we acknowledge. Saint Cyril of Jerusalem and Saint Ambrose of Milan produced such books in the fourth century. Great saints have followed suit. In the last century, many more such books appeared, from authors as great as Monsignor Ronald Knox and Archbishop Fulton Sheen.

Why do Catholics need new books to go over the same ground? Saint Augustine addressed God as a truth "ever ancient and ever new." The prayers and signs do come to us from venerable antiquity, and they remain basically the same. Yet some details change, as the rites make their home in different times and cultures. We've changed, and so our experience of the Mass has changed. It's time for us to take a fresh look, from where we sit now—and from where we stand and kneel.

ONE

WHAT MAKES THE MASS: PEOPLE, PLACES, WORDS, AND THINGS

The Beginnings in the Bible

THE ORIGINS OF THE MASS are found in Jesus' Last Supper, which we can read about in three of the Gospels (Matthew, Mark, and Luke) as well as one of the New Testament letters of Saint Paul (1 Corinthians). Even people who have never read the Bible know the story because of the famous artworks that depict the moment. Probably the most famous is by Leonardo da Vinci. Leonardo's image places Christ at the center, with the elements of bread and wine, as the apostles flank him on either side. Reproductions and imitations appear in many churches, as well as in the homes of Catholics around the world. It has long been a custom to hang such a picture in the family dining room, to remind us that every meal should be a reflection of that most important meal in all history.

What took place there, in that room, is the mystery at the heart of every Mass.

The night before he died, Jesus gathered his apostles with him to celebrate the Passover meal, a traditional Jewish sacrificial meal. The Passover was a solemn feast dedicated to the remembrance of Israel's deliverance from slavery in Egypt. As God prepared the nation of Israel for the Exodus, he sent a plague that claimed the life of every firstborn son in Egypt. The firstborn sons of Israel were spared because they observed the ritual prescribed by God through Moses. Each household sacrificed a lamb and consumed it with other foods (all rich in symbolism), including unleavened bread and wine. The lamb was offered to God in place of the *life* God had demanded, the life of the firstborn son.

When Israel became established in the land promised by God, they customarily marked the Passover in Jerusalem, the nation's capital and holy city.

In the time of Jesus, devout Jews came, by the hundreds of thousands, from all over the known world to mark the day in Jerusalem. In the prescribed prayers and readings of Passover, the family recalled the Exodus as if it were a current event, as if their deliverance were taking place in their own generation. They also looked forward to a definitive

The Last Supper is an image captured in both humble and ornate art throughout the centuries. © *Michael Hoyt*

deliverance, when a Messiah, an anointed king, would establish God's kingdom in its fullness and bring peace to the chosen people.

This was the context for Jesus' Last Supper. He said to his twelve apostles: "I have eagerly desired to eat this Passover with you before I suffer" (Luke 22:15).

In the course of the meal, he took the bread and he declared it to be his body and then he took the cup of wine and he declared it to be his blood. All of this he did in fulfillment of something that he had promised in his preaching.

In the sixth chapter of John's Gospel, we first see Jesus multiplying loaves to feed a multitude. That bread, however, served as a sign of something greater. For, afterward, we find Jesus reflecting on the "bread of life," the "bread that comes down from heaven"—a bread that would be his "flesh for the life of the world," a bread that would be "true food" while his blood was "true drink."

The crowd that heard him found his words to be strange and many people left him that day.

Yet all those words came to fulfillment the night before Jesus died. Certainly the Twelve remembered that Bread of Life discourse when Jesus pronounced those words over the Passover bread and wine: "This is my body. . . . This is the cup of my blood."

With the Last Supper, Jesus inaugurated what Christians have, ever since, called the "Paschal Mystery," the mystery of the suffering, death, and Resurrection of the God-man. We call it "Paschal" because of its beginning at Passover, which is called *Pesach* in Hebrew and *Pascha* in Latin and Greek.

At every Passover, a lamb was offered in place of the

firstborn son. Where is the lamb at this Passover? It is Jesus, whom John the Baptist had proclaimed as the "Lamb of God" (John 1:29). At this new Passover, Jesus offered himself as the perfect sacrifice—the firstborn Son of God offered himself as the definitive Paschal Lamb. As we sing in a popular hymn: "For the sheep the Lamb has bled, / Sinless in the sinner's stead."

Jesus wanted to make this "mystery" a permanent reality, which would be continued for every believer in the years and centuries and millennia after his death and Resurrection. Thus, he charged the apostles, "Do this in remembrance of me."

What we remember in the Eucharist is Christ's sacrifice at Calvary, where he offered himself, laid down his life, for our redemption. The Mass is a real sacrifice because Jesus' self-offering was a real sacrifice. Saint Paul put it well: "For our Paschal Lamb, Christ, has been sacrificed. Therefore let us celebrate the feast . . . with the unleavened bread of sincerity and truth" (1 Corinthians 5:7–8).

Our "remembrance" is not merely a psychological act, a retrieval of data stored away in neurons. Nor is it simply a historical commemoration, whose details are kept alive in old books. No, our remembrance is a *re-presentation* of a unique moment in history. It took place *once,* but *for all.* Now, when we go to Mass, we speak of the Paschal Mystery as a present reality, just as the families of Israel spoke of their deliverance during the Passover ritual. Moreover, because of Jesus' promise, we know that his presence is indeed a *real presence.* He is really there. We are really with him.

Even more than that, we are united with him in a closer

bond than any friendship or merely human love could ever provide. The bread we break is a true communion in Christ's body. Our blessing cup is a true communion in his blood. This is what Saint Paul emphasized in his First Letter to the Corinthians. At Mass, we participate—we share—in Jesus' death and Resurrection through this unique presence that the Church calls "sacramental." It is real, but it is made real through the action of the Holy Spirit in and through the use of sacred signs and symbols. These symbols, by the grace of God, have the power not only to manifest what's happening, but to make it truly happen. They accomplish what they signify. That's the difference between a sacramental sign and any other type of symbol or sign.

In the Mass, Jesus instituted the sacrament through which his Passion, death, and Resurrection would be made present again in our lives. The Eucharist enables each of us to share in the benefits of the cross. We speak of our "dying to sin" and "rising to new life" because we participate in the mystery of Christ's death and Resurrection. The Church uses the word "re-present" to speak of what is happening in the Mass. The term "holy sacrifice" of the Mass is also exact because sacramentally, but really and truly, the death and Resurrection of Christ are once again made present.

Because Jesus is really present in our Communion, we truly become a part of him. We can compare the Mass to a parade. There are two ways you can experience a parade: you can stand on the curb and watch it go by, or you can join the ranks and march along with the band. Marching in a parade is essentially different from watching one go by. Sacramental life means taking our place as God's children and truly sharing in divine life—not just standing on the sidelines and watching Jesus go by, or talking about his passing. That's what the Mass is all about.

Saint Luke tells the great story of what Jesus did on the day he rose from the dead (Luke 24:13–35). He walked with his disciples. He opened up the Scriptures to them. And then he made himself known to them in the breaking of the bread. When that happened, he vanished from their sight. His real presence, then, was not something the physical eyes could see. It was something hidden under the sacramental signs: the appearances of bread and wine.

The early Christians understood all this. In the Acts of the Apostles, we see a thumbnail sketch of the very first days of the very first generation of the Church. What did the Church do then? What did Catholics do?

"They devoted themselves to the teaching of the apostles and to the communal life, to the breaking of the bread and to the prayers" (Acts 2:42). There it is: the first Catholic parish coming together on Sunday. This is what we Catholics still do when we go to Mass. We hear the teaching. We experience communion and fellowship in Christ. We break bread and offer the traditional prayers.

Devout Christians have, since that first generation, marked their Sundays this way. They have also read the Scriptures this way, seeing in the story of the Last Supper and the Bread of Life discourse the origins of the Mass. Yet the Mass is hardly limited to those few texts. We find it explored theologically in the Epistle to the Hebrews, and presented in a visionary way in the Book of Revelation. Saint Paul refers to it often, in passing, as he conducts his correspondence with far-flung churches. We find it, moreover—

as Christians always have—foretold and foreshadowed in the sacred writings of ancient Israel, the Church's Old Testament. In the prayers of the Mass, we recall many of those moments: the sacrifice of Abel, the bread and wine offered by the priest Melchizedek, the "goodness of the Lord" that we can "taste and see."

This is something God foresaw and foreknew, and something he revealed in the fullness of time. Like Christians of every age, we now can see it, too, though in a hidden and mysterious way, in a mystery.

The Mass Through History

FOR CATHOLICS, EVERY MASS IS the same event as the Last Supper. At the Last Supper, "on the night he was betrayed, our Savior instituted the Eucharistic sacrifice of his body and blood." This firmly held teaching of the Church, repeated in the Second Vatican Council's Constitution on the Sacred Liturgy (n. 47), is clearly reaffirmed in the Catechism of the Catholic Church (n. 1323). The origins of the Mass are found in the Last Supper. Not that the ritual meals match up in all the details. They do not. The actions, though, are mystically united. When Jesus commanded his apostles "Do this in memory of me," he gave them the power to extend his sacrifice, and participate in it, for all time.

And so they did. They organized the Christian Church around "the breaking of the bread and the prayers" (Acts 2:42), and they observed the solemn meal, consecrating the same elements—bread and wine—that Jesus had used. Within fifty years of the death of the last apostle, Saint Justin Martyr boasted that the Mass already was celebrated among every race on earth. The earliest Christian writers, Saint Clement of Rome (first century) and Saint Ignatius of Antioch (first and second centuries), discuss the Mass as a well-established institution. It recurs as a major theme in their works. Its doctrine and theology were already well developed. Christians, from the beginning, were expected to know and love the Mass.

The Eucharist was, moreover, considered to be the same throughout the world, whether it was celebrated in Rome or Antioch or Palestine. Yet, by the year A.D. 300, it was already offered in a variety of languages—Greek, Latin, Syriac, Coptic—according to many different local customs. Different cultures enriched the Church's worship with their distinctive traditions of poetry, music, and art. In the first millennium of Christianity, the Church developed several great "liturgical families" or "rites." In the Western Church, as distinguished from the Eastern Catholic Churches, the "Mass" is what we call the liturgy of the Latin Rite, the Church family that found its cultural center in the city of Rome and spread from there to the entire world. Since the Latin Rite is used most extensively throughout the Church in the United States, it is the one we follow in this book.

Some elements of the ceremonies developed over time. Others have remained virtually the same, even to our own day. We'll occasionally discuss the history of individual parts of the Mass as we come to them in this book.

Any history of the Mass that confines itself to one chapter will be necessarily and uncomfortably brief. Many scholarly histories of the Mass actually run to several volumes. We can note here that Latin Rite Catholics have witnessed several periods of great development in their expression of worship. In our own day, we may be living through another of those periods.

The earliest Roman liturgy was probably celebrated in Greek, the common language of commerce and culture in the ancient world. From the late second century onward, however, there was a great flowering of Latin Christian culture, and this surely influenced the Church's liturgy throughout the Western lands: Italy, North Africa, and the lands we now know as Spain and France. Gradually, worship in the West was Latinized. By the late fourth century, the shift seems to be almost complete.

The great councils of the Church issued decrees about the celebration of the Mass, but these tended to treat matters of general concern rather than specifics of the rituals. The early popes contributed their own developments, which tended to be more specific; many of these are duly recorded in the ancient chronicles of the Roman Church.

In the sixth and seventh centuries, Byzantine government exerted a greater influence over the city of Rome; many Greek-speaking Christians migrated to Rome and the surrounding regions, for jobs in government and trade. They brought their customs of worship with them, and some of these found their way into the Roman rites.

Saint Gregory the Great, who reigned as pope from 590 to 604, undertook a great reform of the liturgy, editing texts, adjusting their place in the ritual, and standardizing the rites of the Latin Church.

In those centuries before mass media or electronic communication, however, it was difficult to achieve any commonly recognized and lasting standard. The ritual books were copied out by hand, usually by monks—a slow process, given to variation. The monasteries, in fact, became the great centers of liturgical development in the Middle Ages. According to Saint Benedict of Nursia, the great founder of Western monasticism, the liturgy was the great "work" in the monks' days. Ritual worship, he said, was "God's work." And so the monks gave great attention to the ceremonies, ornamenting them, for example, with their great traditions of chant.

Through the Middle Ages, there was a movement toward standardization of the rite of celebration of the Mass, especially as the countries of Europe worked to achieve more open lines of communication and trade. Saint Francis asked his friars to offer the Mass as it was offered at the papal court; and so Franciscans spread the Roman ritual as they went about their ministry. They also lent mighty efforts to the collection and editing of the rites and their orderly arrangement in books.

With the Protestant Reformation in the sixteenth century, Church discipline broke down in many areas. In some places, would-be reformers took liberties with the ancient texts and rewrote the rites to suit their understanding of theology. The Church found it necessary to enforce uniformity as much as possible—and, because of the advent of the printing press, it was possible to a greater degree than ever before. Acting on a directive of the Council of Trent, Pope Saint Pius V issued an authoritative Roman Missal in 1570. It underwent some corrections and revisions over the next four centuries, but remained substantially the same.

At the beginning of the twentieth century, Pope Saint Pius X encouraged the development of a "Liturgical Movement" in the Church. He urged the clergy to take care with their pronunciation of the Latin words of the Mass. He took a special interest in sacred music and chant. And he encouraged lay Catholics to receive Communion frequently, a practice that had fallen out of fashion in many places.

The Liturgical Movement grew in its influence throughout the twentieth century, and it was one of the great tributaries to the work of the Second Vatican Council (1962–1965). The Council Fathers followed Pope Saint Pius X in seeking greater lay participation in the Mass. They encouraged the translation of the Mass into vernacular languages, and they called for a reform of the Missal, which the Servant of God Pope Paul VI oversaw in the years following the Council. In 1969, he issued the new Roman Missal, which differed in many significant ways from its predecessor: it included several Eucharistic Prayers rather than one, and its lectionary drew far more material from Sacred Scripture.

Pope Paul's Missal has since undergone several revisions. As this book goes to press, the Missal is in its third edition, and its English translation has just been approved. It is that most recent text that appears throughout these pages.

The Missal presents some new words here and there. Yet the reality, the event, is the very same mystery the first disciples encountered when they met with Jesus in an "upper room" in Jerusalem, twenty centuries ago.

Mass: A Word About the Word

THE WORD *MASS* IS ANCIENT indeed. It comes from the Latin noun *Missa,* whose earliest surviving appearance is in the writing of Saint Ambrose, the bishop of Milan, from the year 386. Ambrose used the word in a letter to his sister. He told her how, amid many disturbances in his church, "I remained at my place and began to say Mass." It's clear, from his casual usage, that *Missa* was already well established by then. It probably had been in use since the dawn of Latin Christianity.

It comes from the final words of the Eucharistic liturgy. In Latin, they are: *Ite, missa est*—roughly, "Go, it is the dismissal." (Today our priests say, "Go forth, the Mass is ended," or similar words.)

The English word *Mass,* strictly speaking, applies only to the Eucharist as it is celebrated in the West, the Catholic Church's Latin Rite, whose great cultural and religious center has always been the ancient Church of Rome. The same reality looks and sounds somewhat different in the liturgies of the Eastern Churches, where it is called by other names:

the "Divine Liturgy," for example, or the "Holy Offering." Essentially, however, the action is the same, and it is understood by means of the same biblical doctrine and the same sacred tradition.

Even in the West, the Mass may take a variety of forms, rites, and uses that are approved by the Catholic Church. In this book we have limited our focus. We wish to document the ordinary form of the Mass as it is celebrated in the majority of Catholic parishes today, according to the most recent edition of the Roman Missal.

Just as the word *Mass* has a special significance for Catholics, so do many of the other terms associated with the Mass. In the following chapters, we'll look more closely at those words, too.

Names for the Mass

LIKE THE HUMAN HEART, THE Mass is a source of life; and so, again like the heart, it is something complex and wondrous.

The Mass has natural and supernatural dimensions. It serves men, women, and children of every race, age, class, culture, language, and temperament. It provides consolation, inspiration, edification, strength, a moment for reflection, and a share of divine life.

Any reality that is so rich will naturally end up with many names and synonyms, each emphasizing a different quality. The Mass has gathered many titles throughout the ages, and you'll encounter them often in these pages.

The Eucharist comes from the Greek word for "thanksgiving." Jews in the time of Jesus sometimes used the word *eucharistia* to describe the "thank-offering," a special sacrifice that was celebrated in the Jerusalem Temple. The Gospels use forms of the word to describe Jesus' action when he instituted the Mass: he "gave thanks" (Mark 14:23).

Liturgy is another word that comes from Greek. *Leitourgia* was a workaday word meaning "public work" or "public service." It distinguishes the Mass from private prayer. It belongs to the assembly, to God's people. Forms of the word appear in the original Greek of the New Testament (in Acts 3:2, for example, and Hebrews 8:6) and in the Greek translation of the Old Testament.

The Breaking of the Bread is a plain description of what has happened at every Mass since Jesus' Last Supper. The New Testament tells us that Jesus "took bread, and . . . broke it" before instructing his apostles to do the same. The newborn Church met for "the breaking of the bread" (Acts 2:42).

The Lord's Supper evokes the original setting of the rite, at Jesus' final meal before his arrest. It also brings to mind many other banquets that we read about in the Bible, from "Wisdom's Banquet" (Proverbs 9:1–5) to the "Wedding Feast of the Lamb" (Revelation 19:9).

The Sacrament, or the *Blessed Sacrament,* like all sacraments, is an outward sign instituted by Jesus Christ and entrusted to the Church. Sacraments are signs perceived by the senses, but they signify a divine life that cannot be seen. We taste the familiar flavor of bread and wine, but we receive Jesus. Sacraments are *efficacious* signs—that is, they are not mere symbols; they accomplish the very thing they signify. The sacraments convey God's grace. There are seven sacraments, and the Eucharist, the Mass, is the greatest of them. It is sometimes called "the Sacrament of Sacraments." (See also "Sacred Mysteries," below.)

The Holy Sacrifice is the only sacrifice that saves us and takes away our sins. This is the sacrifice of Jesus, who offered himself on the cross. This took place "once for all" (Hebrews 7:27, 10:10)—"once" in history, but "for all" in the sacrament by which Jesus offered himself, as he said "This is my body." "The sacrifice" was the most commonly used name for the Mass in the early Church. We find it in the Letter to the Hebrews (13:15) and other Scriptures, but also in the earliest writings of the fathers of the Church.

The Sacred Mysteries may at first make us think of "mysteries" in terms of puzzles or unsolved crimes. To the early Christians, however, the Greek word *mysterion* stood for the hidden things of God that Jesus came to reveal. He did this through his suffering, death, and Resurrection (known as the Paschal Mystery). He continues to reveal and to share his divine life through the sacraments. Thus, the Greek *mysterion* is often translated into English as "sacrament."

Preparing for Mass

JESUS SPOKE OF THE MASS and Holy Communion in terms
of necessity: "unless you eat the flesh of the Son of Man and
drink his blood, you do not have life within you. Whoever
eats my flesh and drinks my blood has eternal life, and I will
raise him on the last day" (John 6:53–54). Yet he also told
a parable of those who come to the banquet unprepared. He
spoke of such a person as an invited guest who came dressed
improperly (Matthew 22:11–12). Saint Paul developed this
doctrine further as he exhorted members of his congregation to examine themselves to discern whether they were
properly prepared for Mass (1 Corinthians 11:28).

The Church gives us clear guidance as we prepare ourselves to receive the Lord. What we do is a consequence of
what we believe. If we believe that Jesus is God, and that
he is really present in the Eucharist, then we will make sure
we are well prepared when we go to receive him. The Eucharist is such an extraordinary gift, such a sacred gift, such
a holy and wondrous gift, that we must not take it lightly,

and we need to recognize the obligations we have before receiving Communion.

While anyone may attend Mass, only those who fulfill certain conditions may receive Holy Communion. We'll discuss these conditions briefly. At the end of the chapter, we'll include the "Guidelines for Receiving Holy Communion," published by the United States Conference of Catholic Bishops.

We must be Catholic. Receiving the Eucharist is a sign, a proclamation, that you are a member of the Catholic Church. You have been baptized, and you have remained "in communion" with the Catholic Church—a unity of common beliefs and practices.

To be Catholic is to belong to "the family of faith" (Galatians 6:10), the "household of God" (1 Peter 4:17). The Church is a family so close-knit, and so close to Jesus, that it has always been identified as the "body of Christ" (see 1 Corinthians 12:27 and Ephesians 4:12). Christ has established the rules for the household, and he has given authority over the family to his apostles and their successors, the bishops. We are not free to make up our own rules. The Church does not come into being because a group of relatively like-minded people get together and say, "I'll accept the doctrines I like, and I'll reject the doctrines I don't like." Yes, there are people who do that, but then they are not truly living in communion with the Catholic Church. They lack what Saint Paul would call "the *obedience* of faith" (Romans 1:5 and 16:26).

To belong to the Church means accepting the Church on its own terms, the terms established by Jesus Christ. It requires a recognition of the whole sacramental order, because that is the way Christ made his Church. He established Baptism, Eucharist, and Holy Orders (by which men are ordained to the priesthood). He established marriage to follow a certain natural and supernatural order.

Before we can truthfully say "Amen" to the priest who presents us with the Body of Christ, we must be able to say "yes" to the Church as the Body of Christ. We must *practice* the "obedience of faith." For the Church's unity is in the Eucharist. Saint Paul made the connection very clearly: one bread, one body. "Because the loaf of bread is one, we, though many, are one body, for we all partake of the one loaf" (1 Corinthians 10:17).

The Church that Jesus established—the Body of Christ, the People of God—is structured, visible, and identifiable. The Lord endowed his community with a structure that will remain until the kingdom is fully achieved. He chose the Twelve, with Peter as their head, as the foundation stones of "a new Jerusalem" (see Revelation 21:2, 10). The apostles and the other disciples share in Christ's mission and his power precisely to lead and serve his new body, so that together through works of faith and love the kingdom of God may become manifest in the world.

The Church instituted by Christ is alive through the power of the Holy Spirit; it is both visible and spiritual. The Second Vatican Council explained: "The one mediator, Christ, established and ever sustains here on earth his holy Church, the community of faith, hope, and charity as a visible organization through which he communicates truth and grace to all" (*Lumen Gentium,* n. 8). The Catechism of the Catholic Church adds that this one visible Church is at the same time a "society structured with hierarchical organs and the mystical body of Christ; the visible society and the spiritual community; the earthly Church and the Church endowed with heavenly riches" (CCC n. 771).

Before we can say "Amen" to Holy Communion, we must say "yes" to this Church as Christ established it. We must be able to say "yes" to all that it teaches. Otherwise we cannot honestly say "Amen" to the priest or minister who holds up "The Body of Christ." An "Amen" with reservations is not a true Amen.

As members of the Catholic community, we must live and act within the structure of this community. That means working in solidarity with the bishops—the successors of the apostles—who are given the responsibility to preserve the unity of the Church as they provide leadership, teach, and sanctify.

Like any loving relationship, our discipleship may sometimes require a struggle on our part. We must bend ourselves, in such cases, to cling to the Lord in communion. We must never bend the Gospel, though, or invent a church to suit our changing desires and preferences.

We must be in a state of grace. This means we should be free of any grave sin—any sin that is "mortal," or deadly to the soul (see 1 John 5:16–17). Saint Paul wrote that "whoever eats the bread or drinks the cup of the Lord unworthily will have to answer for the body and blood of the Lord" (1 Corinthians 11:27). A person who approaches Communion in the state of mortal sin "eats and drinks judgment on himself" (11:29). To receive Communion unworthily is to

bring judgment on oneself, not salvation, not the blessing
of God.

It is very important for us, then, to understand what
makes a sin "mortal." The Catechism of the Catholic Church
tells us that "Mortal sin is sin whose object is grave matter
and which is also committed with full knowledge and de-
liberate consent" (CCC n. 1857). "To choose deliberately—
that is, both knowing it and willing it—something gravely
contrary to the divine law and to the ultimate end of man is
to commit a mortal sin" (CCC n. 1874). The Catechism applies the term "mortal" to a wide variety of offenses, some
of them predictable, like murder and grand theft, but also
to extreme anger (see CCC n. 2302) and envy (see CCC
n. 2539).

If we discern the truth of the real presence, we know
instinctively what it says in the Bible's Book of Revelation
(21:27): "nothing unclean will enter" the presence of the
Lamb of God.

The action of the Mass is, by itself, sufficient for the
forgiveness of smaller sins (venial sins). But if we know we
are in a state of mortal sin, we must first go to sacramental
confession before we receive Holy Communion.

The Church believes in the forgiveness of sins. Not only
did Jesus die to wash away all sin—and not only in his public
life did he forgive sin—but after his Resurrection Jesus also
extended to his Church the power to apply the redemption
won on the cross and the authority to forgive sin.

The Catechism points out that our faith in the forgiveness of sins is one with our faith in the Holy Spirit, the
Church, and the communion of saints. "It was when he

gave the Holy Spirit to his apostles that the risen Christ conferred on them his own divine power to forgive sins: 'Receive the Holy Spirit. If you forgive the sins of any, they are forgiven; if you retain the sins of any, they are retained' " (CCC n. 976).

This power to forgive sins is often referred to as the "power of the keys." Saint Augustine pointed out that the Church has "received the keys of the kingdom of heaven so that, in her, sins may be forgiven through Christ's blood and the Holy Spirit's action. In this Church, the soul dead through sin comes back to life in order to live with Christ, whose grace has saved us."

Think of the words of Jesus: "Therefore if you bring your gift at the altar, and there recall that your brother has anything against you, leave your gift there at the altar, go first and be reconciled to your brother, and then come and offer your gift" (Matthew 5:23–24).

There is a tendency, in some quarters, simply to diminish the concept of sin, and say that everybody should receive Communion, because we all need to stay close to God, no matter what we are doing. This attitude ignores the fact that sin is a separation from God and requires a real act of reconciliation.

We must believe in the real presence. Again, to use the words of Saint Paul, we need to "discern the body." The church teaches that the Eucharist is truly the body and the blood of Christ. It is his body and blood made present in a way that *re-presents* his death, now in an unbloody manner, and his Resurrection. This is what Christians have believed since the beginning. In A.D. 107, Saint Ignatius of Antioch wrote:

"I have no taste for corruptible food nor for the pleasures of this life. I desire the bread of God, which is the flesh of Jesus Christ, who was of the seed of David; and for drink I desire his blood, which is love incorruptible." He said that the most visible mark of the heretics was that "they do not confess the Eucharist to be the flesh of our Savior Jesus Christ, flesh that suffered for our sins and which the Father, in his goodness, raised up again."

If someone today finds that teaching unacceptable, then they really are not free to present themselves for Communion.

We must fast for one hour. The Church asks us to observe a fast from food and beverages for one hour preceding our Holy Communion. It is a small sacrifice, and much of the hour is taken up with the Mass anyway. The custom goes back to ancient times, though even very recently the duration of the fast was much longer—from midnight the night before. Water never breaks the fast. Neither does medicine. We should avoid chewing candies or gum during the Mass, as it is impolite to do so at any banquet, much less the banquet of the King of Kings.

We should tend to the small details. We should dress appropriately and modestly. Dress respectably, and not in any way that will draw attention to yourself rather than the Mass.

We should arrive on time or, if possible, a little early. When you arrive late, you may distract others. Still, it is far better to arrive late than not arrive at all.

We should plan to remain until the very end. Don't make appointments for immediately after Mass, unless it's absolutely necessary to do so. Give yourself completely to the Lord for this little bit of time.

We should shut off cell phones, pagers, and other communications devices. We should silence the alarm tones on our watches. Leave earth for heaven, if only for this moment. Yes, some people need to be reachable—doctors on call, for example, and people who are caring for a critically ill family member. But most of us, most of the time, can afford to tune out the noise of the world for an hour or so. It will improve the quality of our prayer.

Guidelines for Receiving Holy Communion
The United States Conference of Catholic Bishops

For Catholics

As Catholics, we fully participate in the celebration of the Eucharist when we receive Holy Communion. We are encouraged to receive Communion devoutly and frequently. In order to be properly disposed to receive Communion, participants should not be conscious of grave sin and normally should have fasted for one hour. A person who is conscious of grave sin is not to receive the Body and Blood of the Lord without prior sacramental confession except for a grave reason where there is no opportunity for confession. In this case, the person is to be mindful of the obligation to make an act of perfect contrition, including the intention of confessing as soon as possible (Can. 916). A frequent reception of the Sacrament of Penance is encouraged for all.

For Our Fellow Christians

We welcome our fellow Christians to this celebration of the Eucharist as our brothers and sisters. We pray that our common baptism and the action of the Holy Spirit in this Eucharist will draw us closer to one another and begin to dispel the sad divisions which separate us. We pray that these will lessen and finally disappear, in keeping with Christ's prayer for us "that they may all be one" (John 17:21).

Because Catholics believe that the celebration of the Eucharist is a sign of the reality of the oneness of faith, life, and worship, members of those churches with whom we are not yet fully united are ordinarily not admitted to Holy Communion. Eucharistic sharing in exceptional circumstances by other Christians requires permission according to the directives of the diocesan bishop and the provisions of canon law (Can. 844 § 4). Members of the Orthodox Churches, the Assyrian Church of the East, and the Polish National Catholic Church are urged to respect the discipline of their own Churches. According to Roman Catholic discipline, the Code of Canon Law does not object to the reception of Communion by Christians of these Churches (Can. 844 § 3).

For Those Not Receiving Holy Communion

All who are not receiving Holy Communion are encouraged to express in their hearts a prayerful desire for unity with the Lord Jesus and with one another.

For Non-Christians

We also welcome to this celebration those who do not share our faith in Jesus Christ. While we cannot admit them to Holy Communion, we ask them to offer their prayers for the peace and the unity of the human family.

The Essentials: Bread and Wine

YOU NEED NOT GO TO one of the world's great cathedrals to be impressed by the ceremony of the Mass. The Church's ritual instructions—called rubrics—call for precious metals, a wardrobe of bright vestments, and some very poetic prayers and chants. Many parishes go further still and adorn the precious metals with jewels, the vestments with embroidery, the austere chants with soaring polyphonic music.

That is all to the good. The Mass—even when it's celebrated in humble surroundings with just a few worshippers—is the greatest event in history, the greatest event imaginable. So it's only natural for Christians to want to give it their best.

Think of the story of King David in the Old Testament. He had triumphed over his enemies, united his people, and built himself a palace. Then: "After David had taken up residence in his house, he said to Nathan the prophet, 'See, I am living in a house of cedar, but the ark of the covenant of the Lord dwells under tentcloth.' Nathan replied to David,

'Do, therefore, whatever you desire, for God is with you' "
(1 Chronicles 17:1–2).

So Catholics throughout history, whether rich or poor,
have indulged the same holy desire by building beautiful
churches, training choirs, and sculpting altars out of blocks
of the hardest granite and the most expressive marble.

All of that is surely pleasing to God, and it makes the
faith more humanly attractive as well. Yet it is not essential. The essence of the rite is bound up in a few words
and actions. All that is necessary (strictly speaking) for the
priest is a bit of bread and a few drops of wine. Indeed,
there are many stories from recent history of priests impris-
oned for their faith—under Nazi and communist regimes—
who "made do" in minimal time with the barest of elements. In some cases they fermented their own wine from
juice they had squeezed out of the few grapes in their prison
rations.

The vessels and furnishings, in times of emergency, may
be dispensed. Many of the prayers may be omitted. The
Catechism (n. 1412) shows us the heart of the matter:

> The essential signs of the Eucharistic sacrament are
> wheat bread and grape wine, on which the blessing of
> the Holy Spirit is invoked and the priest pronounces
> the words of consecration spoken by Jesus during the
> Last Supper: "This is my body which will be given up
> for you. . . . This is the cup of my blood."

Unleavened wheat bread and simple wine: these are two
of the elements in the Passover meal that Jesus celebrated.

All the accounts, in the Bible and in other early Christian writings, agree on these two elements.

The host—this word comes from the Latin word describing a sacrificial victim. People sometimes speak colloquially of hosts that are "consecrated" or "unconsecrated," depending on whether or not they have been used (and thus transformed) in the Mass. But, strictly speaking, the Church refers to the unconsecrated wafers as "altar breads." Only after consecration may we truly speak of a sacrificial victim, a "host." The altar breads must be made of wheat flour and water, with no additives. In the Western Church we use thin, round unleavened wafers.

The wine must be made from grapes, fermented, with no flavors or additives, and must be unspoiled. (A priest who is alcoholic may obtain permission to use a wine that is only a bit fermented, called *mustum*.) During the Mass, at the preparation of the gifts, a small amount of water is added to the wine.

Simple wheat bread and grape wine: they were the basic ingredients of any festive meal in Jesus' culture, in the ancient Mediterranean world. We may not substitute any elements for these. The question has come up throughout history, when the Gospel spread to societies that were more dependent on other grains and fruits. But the church has always ruled that we are obligated to preserve the type in the matter of the sacraments. The Word became flesh in a particular time and place. He entered a particular history, and observed a particular people's festival: the Passover. We must never obscure that fact.

The elements may be simple, common, plain, and basic. Yet they are rich in all they signify. Grape wine (at least when it's red) suggests the saving blood of Jesus Christ. When mixed with water, it evokes the two fluids that poured from his side on the cross. Wine, according to the Scriptures, gladdens the spirit (see Psalms 104:15; Ecclesiastes 9:7); and so, in a supreme and everlasting way, does the sacrament.

The Bible equates bread with the continuation of life. A family could not survive without its daily bread. Material bread sustains us, draws the family together around the table, and satisfies. How much more the bread come down from heaven (see John 6).

A Word About Obligation

CATHOLICS HAVE A DUTY TO attend Mass on Sundays and other holy days indicated by the Church. We may also fulfill our obligation by attending Mass on the eve, or vigil, of the holy day—on Saturday for the Sunday obligation. To miss Mass without good reason—illness, for example, or care for a homebound family member—is to commit a grave sin.

The Church does not ask us to do the impossible. If there is no Mass available within a reasonably accessible distance, we are excused from our duty. Sometimes, too, a bishop may dispense Catholics from their obligation because of inclement weather or other extreme circumstances.

Still, we should try always to plan our Sundays with Mass in mind. We should make Mass attendance a key element, for example, in our travel itineraries and vacation plans. Diocesan websites sometimes link to Mass times in all their parishes; these resources can be very helpful.

This law of the Church imposes a sweet obligation. The Church commands us to do something that will benefit us anyway! The Sunday obligation is a "duty" to draw near to God, experience Christ's love, and worship him in a beautiful way.

We should strive to have the attitude of the Christians of Abitina, a church in North Africa. In A.D. 304, Roman persecutors rounded up a group of them who had gathered for worship. At their trial, the judge asked them why they had exposed themselves to such danger. They replied: "We cannot live without Sunday Mass!"

True heroes, they preferred the Mass to safety and security. We should at least prefer it to our pastimes and pleasures.

The Catechism of the Catholic Church on the Sunday Obligation

The Sunday Eucharist is the foundation and confirmation of all Christian practice. For this reason the faithful are obliged to participate in the Eucharist on days of obligation, unless excused for a serious reason (for example, illness, the care of infants) or dispensed by their own pastor. Those who deliberately fail in this obligation commit a grave sin (n. 2181).

The Code of Canon Law on the Sunday Obligation

Sunday . . . is to be observed as the foremost holy day of obligation in the universal Church (1246 § 1).

The Parts of the Mass

THE MASS IS DIVIDED INTO two main parts: (1) the Liturgy of the Word and (2) the Liturgy of the Eucharist. The first part focuses on the proclamation of God's Word, as it is revealed in the Scriptures. The second part is the celebration of the memorial itself, the remembrance of Christ's Passion, death, and Resurrection. These two main sections of the Mass are further divided into several parts—prayers and groups of prayers called "rites"—each of which will receive its own chapter in this book.

On a typical Sunday, the first "half" of the Mass, the Liturgy of the Word, begins with the "introductory rite," which consists of prayerful greetings and invocations of Almighty God. This is followed by a "Penitential Rite," in which we recite prayers that express sorrow for our sins. We proceed then to sing or recite the *Gloria,* an ancient hymn of praise, which begins, "Glory to God in the highest!" Then, after the priest offers a brief prayer, we hear readings from several books of the Bible. In his homily, the priest will comment on the readings and apply them to our lives.

After the homily, we profess the creed, which is a summary of basic Christian beliefs. Then we respond to some brief prayers of petition.

The second "half," the Liturgy of the Eucharist, is the very heart of the Mass. In the early Church, only baptized Christians in good standing were permitted to stay for this portion of the Mass. It begins with a collection of "gifts" from the congregation. We put our envelopes in the collection basket. Then these gifts are brought to the altar with gifts of bread and wine. During the Eucharistic Prayer, the priest offers the bread and wine to God. They become the body and blood of Christ. Our gifts to God become God's greatest gift to us. During the Communion rite, this gift is distributed to us. In Holy Communion, we receive the body and blood, soul and divinity of Jesus Christ. After Communion, the priest cleanses the vessels, and we are hastily dismissed.

It's interesting to note how consistently the Church has celebrated the Mass, down the centuries. There is no better illustration of this fact than the section of the Catechism of the Catholic Church titled "The Mass of All Ages" (beginning with n. 1345). When the Church wanted to describe the Mass in our own time, it could do no better than to present, verbatim, a text written by Saint Justin Martyr around A.D. 155. In a letter to the pagan Emperor Antoninus Pius, Justin described the Mass as it was celebrated in the city of Rome, and we can already see both the whole and its parts.

On the day we call the day of the sun, all who dwell in the city or country gather in the same place.

The memoirs of the apostles and the writings of the prophets are read, as much as time permits.

When the reader has finished, he who presides over those gathered admonishes and challenges them to imitate these beautiful things.

Then we all rise together and offer prayers for ourselves . . . and for all others, wherever they may be, so that we may be found righteous by our life and actions, and faithful to the commandments, so as to obtain eternal salvation.

When the prayers are concluded we exchange the kiss.

Then someone brings bread and a cup of water and wine mixed together to him who presides over the brethren.

He takes them and offers praise and glory to the Father of the universe, through the name of the Son and of the Holy Spirit and for a considerable time he gives thanks [in Greek: *eucharistian*] that we have been judged worthy of these gifts.

When he has concluded the prayers and thanksgivings, all present give voice to an acclamation by saying: "Amen."

When he who presides has given thanks and the people have responded, those whom we call deacons give to those present the "Eucharisted" bread, wine and water and take them to those who are absent.

Writing in those years so close to the time of the apostles, Justin is an important witness to the beliefs and practices of the first Christians. He shows us that they marked each Sunday by going to Mass, and that their Mass included readings from the Scriptures, a sermon, prayers of petition, a Eucharistic Prayer, a Sign of Peace, a great Amen, and a Communion—followed by "Communion calls" to people who are sick and homebound. It is a Mass in which we could feel at home, even though we look back at it from a distance of almost two thousand years. Much has changed in Western culture, but the Mass remains the Mass.

Through those two thousand years, saints and scholars have proposed many ways to contemplate the Mass and its parts.

Some have pondered the ritual of the Mass as a kind of symbolic re-enactment of the historical events in the Gospels. Jesus' life began with an overshadowing of the Spirit, at the Annunciation to Mary (see Luke 1:28). So, at the beginning of Mass, the priest echoes the words of the angel as he says: "The Lord be with you"; and the people respond, "And with your spirit." A typical Sunday Mass then proceeds to the prayer that begins "Glory to God in the highest," which is based on the angels' hymn at the first Christmas (Luke 2:14). The proclamation of the readings, then, corresponds to Jesus' public ministry. The Liturgy of the Eucharist corresponds to his sacrifice: his Passion, death, and Resurrection.

Others have emphasized the heavenly aspects of the Church's worship. We begin the Mass by acknowledging the presence of "all the angels and saints" as we confess our sins. We sing of God's glory in highest heaven, and we join the song that the angels sing in heaven: "Holy, holy, holy" (see Isaiah 6:3 and Revelation 4:8). In the great Eucharistic Prayer, we mark the union of heaven and earth, as the whole Church on earth joins with the angels to give praise and thanks to God.

While these ways of interpreting the Mass—spiritual and allegorical—are hallowed by the lives and writings of the saints, they all presume a solid grounding in the literal, historical, and doctrinal senses of the prayers and gestures. (This book, because it's an introduction, focuses on these latter, basic senses.)

There are probably as many ways to love the Mass as there are Christians at worship with us each Sunday. In the Mass, the saints have found an infinity of riches, a reality that can be seen anew from many angles. Each of its parts, moreover, is a point of entry for richer contemplation.

The Mass at a Glance: Outline of a Typical
Sunday Mass in Ordinary Time

The Liturgy of the Word

    Introductory Rite
        Antiphon or song
        Sign of the Cross
        Greeting
    Penitential Rite
        "I Confess" and/or "Lord, Have Mercy"
    Gloria
    Opening Prayer
    First Reading (usually from the Old Testament)
    Responsorial Psalm

Second Reading (usually from the New Testament
     letters)
Alleluia and Gospel Reading
Homily
Creed
General Intercessions (prayers of petition)

The Liturgy of the Eucharist

Preparation of the Altar and the Gifts
Collection
Presentation of Bread and Wine
Prayer over the Gifts
Preface
"Holy, Holy, Holy"
Eucharistic Prayer
Communion Rite
     The Lord's Prayer ("Our Father")
     The Sign of Peace
     "Lamb of God" and Breaking of the Bread
     Communion
Cleansing of Vessels
Closing Prayer
Blessing and Dismissal

The People at Mass and Their Roles

THE MASS IS A GATHERING. It is never a solitary act—because, even if a priest celebrates without a congregation, he does so, nevertheless, in the presence of God and all the angels and saints of heaven.

Jesus himself has a manifold presence at every Mass.

Above all, Jesus is present—really, truly, substantially—in the Eucharist. There he abides in his body, blood, soul, and divinity.

He is present also in the Word proclaimed from the Bible, since it is his Word, divinely inspired. The New Testament speaks of the Scriptures as being "breathed" by God (see 2 Timothy 3:16).

Jesus is present in his people, too—in the Church, the assembly, the congregation. Saint Paul often wrote of the Church as Christ's body (see, for example, 1 Corinthians 12:13 and Ephesians 4:4–16).

Christ is present also in the person of the priest. In fact, it is Christ who offers the Mass, though he does so through the ministry of the priest. By the sacrament of Holy Orders, a priest is conformed to Christ in a special way, and so he can act in Christ's name. The priest offers the Mass, and it is truly Christ offering the Mass. The priest forgives sins, and it is truly Christ forgiving the sins.

Without an *ordained priest,* the Mass is impossible. In the New Testament, we see that, while all believers were equal, they played many different roles in the Church; and they fulfilled these roles in response to God's call. Some were ordained for ministry by the "laying on of hands" (see Acts 13:3); this is the sacrament of Holy Orders. It is this "ordination" that confers the power and grace that enables a priest to offer the Mass.

The priest is called the *celebrant* of the Mass, because it is he who celebrates the feast, he who offers the sacrifice. Sometimes (usually on special occasions) more than one priest or bishop may celebrate together. That is called *concelebrating* the Mass.

Though a priest may celebrate Mass privately, the Mass is the Church's ordinary form of public worship. So it is, most of the time, celebrated with a *congregation.* The Church is a priestly people, and so the lay members also make an offering at Mass. They offer the world to God, because God has given humanity stewardship and dominion over the earth (Genesis 1:28). In the prayer of their hearts, the worshippers put everything they have on the altar. They offer it all to God. This is how the Church expresses the laity's participation at Mass: "For their work, prayers and apostolic endeavors, their ordinary married and family life, their daily labor, their mental and physical relaxation, if carried out in the Spirit, and even the hardships of life if patiently borne—all of these become spiritual sacrifices acceptable to

The laying on of hands has been a part of the ordination of a priest since the beginning of Christianity (see Acts 13:3). © *Paul Fetters*

God through Jesus Christ (see 1 Peter 2:5). During the celebration of the Eucharist these sacrifices are most lovingly offered to the Father along with the Lord's body. Thus as worshippers whose every deed is holy, the lay faithful consecrate the world itself to God" (from *Lumen Gentium,* n. 34, of the Second Vatican Council).

Sometimes, another kind of cleric may take part in the Mass: the *deacon.* The Church ordains deacons to assist bishops and priests in their ministry, in particular the ministry of charity. A deacon may call the congregation to prayer, proclaim the Gospel, preach a homily, prepare the altar for the Eucharist, and/or help with the distribution of Holy Communion.

A *lector* is someone who may proclaim the first and second Scripture readings in the Liturgy of the Word. (In this book, we use the word *lector* to refer to someone appointed,

Deacons assist bishops and priests in their ministry, including proclaiming the Gospel. © *Paul Fetters*

usually by the pastor, to read at Mass. The term can also refer to an instituted ministry in the Church, usually conferred upon men preparing for priestly ministry.) The power to proclaim and preach the Gospel comes with the Sacrament of Holy Orders, so only a bishop, priest, or deacon may read the Gospel during Mass or preach a homily.

A *cantor* may lead the congregation in parts of the Mass that are chanted or sung—for example, the Responsorial Psalm.

Altar servers, or *acolytes,* are children, youth, or adults who assist with various parts of the Mass: for example, lighting and carrying candles, bearing a processional cross, bringing the gifts of bread and wine to the altar, holding the ritual books (that contain the prayers), and ringing bells at appropriate times.

Extraordinary ministers of Holy Communion are members of

The lector proclaims the first and second Scripture readings. © *Paul Fetters*

the Church, specially trained and authorized, who help the priest to distribute the Eucharist, either at Mass or in visits to shut-ins. (This title is sometimes abbreviated, in everyday speech, as "Eucharistic ministers." It's easier to say, but can lead to confusion, as the clergy are the "ordinary" ministers of Holy Communion.)

Ushers greet worshippers, show them to a seat, collect the congregation's contributions at the offertory, keep an orderly queue for Holy Communion, and carry out other tasks as directed by their pastor.

The *choir,* musicians, and soloists glorify God by performing sacred music, composed specifically for worship.

The Church and Its Furnishings

CATHOLIC CHURCHES COME IN A wide variety of shapes, sizes, and architectural styles. They share some things in common, however. The two main parts are the *sanctuary* and the *nave*.

The *sanctuary* is an area set apart for the altar, distinct from the rest of the church. The word *sanctuary* literally means "holy place." It is where almost all the rites of the Mass take place.

The *nave* is the main body of the church, where the worshippers gather. The word comes from the Latin word for ship (*navis*). The early Christians liked to compare the Church to a ship. To them, the Church was Saint Peter's boat, where Christ was present and could teach his people (see Luke 5:3). They often built their churches to resemble a ship.

The *altar* is the focal point of the church's furnishings. An altar is different from an ordinary table. A table is for a meal or banquet, and the Mass is certainly a meal and a banquet, but the Mass is still more than that. It is a *sacrifice*. An altar is a furnishing made specifically for sacrifice. The altar is the place where the sacrificial death and the Resurrection of Christ will be sacramentally renewed.

A chair stands near the altar, and is often flanked by other chairs. The prominent chair is the *presider's chair,* which belongs to the priest. It symbolizes his place as the "head" of Christ's body, the Church, in the congregation gathered for worship.

A *crucifix*—that is, an image of Jesus on the cross—stands visibly near the altar. The crucifix may be a painting or sculpture. Or it may be a processional cross that is carried in at the beginning of Mass. The crucifix reminds us of what is taking place on that altar, what is being done, as Jesus said, "in remembrance." The Mass, like the Last Supper, makes present the one sacrifice of Christ on the cross.

Candles are placed on or near the altar. Since the emergence of electric light, these have a purely symbolic purpose: they symbolize Jesus Christ, the "light of the world" (John 8:12). A large candle, called the Paschal Candle, usually stands near the altar. It is lit for Masses in the Easter season and for Masses of Christian Burial. Candles used for the Mass are traditionally made (mostly) of beeswax, which is noted for its purity and clean burning. The ancients saw in beeswax a symbol of the pure flesh of Jesus Christ.

The *ambo* or *pulpit* is the lectern from which the Scriptures are proclaimed and the homily preached.

Kneelers or cushions are usually provided at all seats in a Catholic church, as the Mass requires worshippers to kneel for certain prayers. Kneeling is a traditional posture for prayer in Western culture, as symbolically rich now as it was in biblical times (see, for example, Luke 22:41 and Acts 20:36).

On entering a church, we'll often find some form of *holy-water font* (sometimes called a "stoup"). We dip our fingers in the water, and then draw it over our body as we make the Sign of the Cross. The action reminds us of our baptism

A crucifix stands visibly near the altar as a reminder
of what is taking place on the altar, as Jesus said,
"in remembrance." © *Paul Fetters*

The tabernacle is the place where consecrated hosts remaining
from the Mass are kept, and should be in a prominent place
in the church. © *Paul Fetters*

and so renews our commitment to Jesus Christ. Holy water is blessed for this prayerful purpose by a priest.

The *sacristy* is a room, usually close to the altar, where the vessels, vestments, and furnishings for Mass are kept. This is where the priest puts on his vestments. Sometimes there is a separate sacristy for people who serve in other liturgical ministries, such as altar servers or the choir.

The *tabernacle* is the repository where the church reserves whatever consecrated hosts are remaining from the Mass. These hosts will be distributed to people who are homebound or hospitalized. Since we believe that Jesus' presence is abiding, we give due reverence to the tabernacle. We genuflect—that is, kneel on our right knee—when we pass the tabernacle. (If our health makes this difficult, we may bow or make some other gesture of reverence.) The tabernacle should be in a conspicuous place in the church, so that people may pray before it. It must also be securely locked, immovable, and made of non-transparent material, so that the sacrament cannot be stolen or desecrated.

The word *tabernacle* literally means "tent," and it calls to mind the tent where God made himself present to the tribes of Israel in their wanderings. When the Gospel speaks of the Incarnation of Jesus, it says, "the Word became flesh and made his dwelling among us" (John 1:14). The phrase may literally be rendered, he "pitched his tent" or "tabernacled among us." In the Mass, the Word becomes flesh for our sake, and he remains present, tabernacled among us.

The *sanctuary lamp* is a special candle that burns perpetually near the tabernacle when the Blessed Sacrament is in reservation, to indicate the presence of Jesus.

The Books

SEVERAL *RITUAL BOOKS* MAY BE used in the Mass. The two basic books are the *lectionary* and the *sacramentary*. The contents of both books, taken together, comprise the *Roman Missal*.

The lectionary is the book that contains the Scripture readings for each day. At each Sunday Mass, there is an assigned first reading (usually from the Old Testament), a Responsorial (usually from the Psalms), a second reading (usually from the New Testament), and a reading from the Gospels. The readings unfold in a three-year cycle. A Catholic who attends Mass regularly will, over the course of three years, hear almost the entire Bible proclaimed.

The sacramentary is the volume of prayers used by the priest or bishop who presides at the Mass. It includes the basic, standard prayers as well as variations for seasons, feast days, and other occasions. Along with the prayers, the sacramentary provides rubrics, or instructions for the priest's position, gestures, and even the volume of his voice. The word *rubric* comes from the Latin word for "red," which is the color of type often used to set these instructions apart from the words of the prayers (usually printed in black).

Sometimes, the bishop, priest, or deacon may read the Gospel passage from a separate liturgical book compiled for that purpose: a *Book of the Gospels.*

The Roman Missal is the book of prayers and blessings used by the priest in the Mass. Some prayers remain the same from week to week. Others change weekly or with the feasts and seasons of the Church's year.

The Roman Missal and the Book of the Gospels are official liturgical books. They are considered sacred items. Thus, they are sometimes beautifully bound and decorated, and always to be treated with reverence.

Those are the official books of the Church. A parish may also make available smaller *pew missals* (or seasonal "missalettes"), which enable worshippers to follow the basic prayers and readings. These smaller publications often include the texts and music for popular hymns as well, though many parishes also distribute separate *hymnals,* too.

Vessels and Cloths

GOD'S PEOPLE HAVE ALWAYS TAKEN special care with the vessels used in their worship. The Israelites fashioned their sacrificial plates, chalices, pitchers, and bowls "of pure gold" (Exodus 37:16). The newborn Church followed this edifying example, and many of the artifacts that survive from the first Christian millennium are vessels used in the Mass. Catholics still devote great care to the creation and upkeep of the altar's accoutrements. The vessels and cloths are to serve, after all, as thrones of Christ the King, who is really present in the Eucharist.

The *paten* is a plate, usually made of precious metal—silver or gold, or it's at least gold-plated. The paten holds the bread that will become the body of Christ.

The *chalice* is a cup made of precious metal to hold the wine, mixed with water, which will become the blood of Christ. These vessels are distinctive, and usually have a stem separating the cup from its base. Like the paten, the chalice is usually beautifully designed. They should be fitting ves-

A chalice is a cup made of precious metal that holds
the wine, mixed with water, that will become the
blood of Christ. © *Paul Fetters*

The ciborium is made of noble or precious metal and
is used to hold the Eucharistic hosts. It often has a lid
for storage in the tabernacle. The chalice and
ciborium pictured were used by Pope Benedict XVI
at Mass at Nationals Park when he visited
Washington, D.C. © *Paul Fetters*

sels constructed from noble materials, the best we can offer, to hold the body and blood of Christ.

A *ciborium* (plural, *ciboria*) is a vessel used to hold the Eucharistic hosts. It is made of noble or precious metal, and it usually has a lid for storage in the tabernacle. Ciboria come in a variety of shapes and styles—some look like bowls and some like chalices.

A *pyx* is a small metal container used to transport consecrated hosts for distribution outside the Mass. It often has the appearance of a pocket watch.

A *chalice veil* may be used to drape the vessels when they are not in use.

The *altar cloth* is like a linen tablecloth that covers the surface of the altar. All the cloths used at the altar are con-

After the offertory, the altar, which is covered in
an altar cloth, is set up for the preparation of the gifts. On the altar
cloth is a corporal, sacramentary, paten with large host, purificator,
chalice, and ciborium. © *Paul Fetters*

sidered sacred items, because they may come in contact with the body and blood of Christ.

The *corporal* is comparable to a place mat in a table setting. It is a square of absorbent white linen that lies flat upon the altar cloth, so that any particles of the host that fall can be collected at the end of Mass. It must be large enough that the paten, chalice, and ciboria may be placed upon it. The word comes from the Latin *corpus,* which means "body."

The *purificator* is a smaller piece of absorbent linen cloth, used to wipe the brim of the chalice after someone has received from it. The purificator is also used to cleanse the inside of the chalice when it is cleaned after Communion.

The *lavabo* is a bowl or small basin used to catch the water when the priest washes his hands at the preparation of the gifts. The word comes from the Latin verb meaning "I shall wash."

Two *cruets* hold wine and water for mixture in the chalice.

The *credence table* is a small piece of furniture near the altar, used to hold the things needed for Mass—such as the cruets and lavabo.

The *censer* or *thurible* is a vessel used for burning incense (optional during Mass). The fragrant smoke represents the prayer of the Church: "Let my prayer be incense before you" (Psalms 141:2).

Vestments

DURING THE MASS, THE PRIEST wears special clothing, called "vestments," which are quite unlike ordinary garments. They remind us of clothes from ancient times, and they signify the priest's role in the Church. He is not there to act in his own name or speak for himself. He is there to stand in the place of Christ. He "puts on Christ" (see Galatians 3:27) like a garment.

When Catholic priests vest themselves, they follow a long tradition. The earliest Christian historians recorded that the apostles did this, too, adopting the vestments of the priests of the Jerusalem Temple. The third-century historian Eusebius tells us that Saint John wore the high priest's insignia on his forehead. Saint Jerome notes that the apostle Saint James always wore the linen vestments reserved for Temple service.

The color of the priest's vestments varies according to the feasts and seasons. Violet or purple is used during Advent and Lent, to symbolize penance. Red sometimes signifies blood (as on Good Friday and the memorials of martyrs

When celebrating Mass, a priest wears an alb, a long white
garment that is put on over his street clothes, and a stole,
which is a long, narrow strip of cloth that symbolizes the priest's
sacramental power as he represents Jesus Christ. © *Paul Fetters*

The outer garment a priest wears is called a chasuble. © *Paul Fetters*

and apostles) and sometimes the fire of the Holy Spirit (as on Pentecost or at a so-called Red Mass for lawyers). Green is used in Ordinary Time, to symbolize life and hope. White vestments are worn on some feasts dedicated to Jesus (like Christmas and Easter), to the Blessed Virgin Mary, to the angels, and to saints who aren't martyrs.

The basic vestments, however, remain the same. They're worn in layers.

The *alb* is the foundation, the vestment the priest puts on over his street clothes. It's a long white garment that reaches to the feet. In the Bible, a white garment is a symbol of purity. Think of the "bright, clean linen garment" that, in the Book of Revelation (19:8), "represents the righteous deeds of the holy ones." Think of Jesus' promise that his faithful ones "will walk with me dressed in white, because they are worthy. The victor will thus be dressed in white" (Revelation 3:4–5). The word *alb* comes from the Latin word for white, *alba*.

The *cincture* is a braided cord, which is drawn as a belt around the alb at the waist.

The *stole* is a long, narrow strip of cloth, sometimes embroidered, that hangs around the neck and down the front of the alb. The stole symbolizes the priest's sacramental power as he represents Jesus Christ. It the Savior's "yoke" that the priest has accepted (see Matthew 11:29–30).

The *chasuble* is the outer vestment the priest wears at Mass. Some historians trace its origins to a sort of sleeveless poncho that was worn by shepherds in ancient times. They could use it almost as a shelter, a tent. As a vestment, then, the chasuble would symbolize the priest's role as a leader, after the Good Shepherd (see John 10:11, 14).

The Church's Calendar

GOD CREATED THE WORLD, AND he made it good (Genesis 1:31). In making material things, God made time as well, for time measures the changes in material things. From the beginning, time followed a holy rhythm. God made the seventh day to be holy, a day set apart, a day of rest and worship. Throughout the Old Testament, we find God's chosen people celebrating feasts of the Lord (see, for example, Leviticus 23:41), preeminently Passover. The Church was born on one of those great feasts of the Jewish calendar, the feast of Pentecost (see Acts 2).

Jesus accomplished our salvation during Passover; and the mystery of our salvation has, ever since, borne the name of that holiday: the Paschal Mystery.

The first Christians rearranged all the passage of time around that reality. As Jews they had faithfully observed the Sabbath on the seventh day of every week; but now, as Christians, they kept "the first day of the week" (Acts 20:7) as "the Lord's Day" (Revelation 1:10). It was the first day, but they also called it the "eighth day." It was both the beginning of their week and its end and fulfillment, just as Jesus is both the beginning and fulfillment of all history (see Revelation 1:8 and 17; 2:8; 21:6).

The Christians marked their holy day on the day Jesus rose from the dead. As Saint Justin Martyr noted for his Roman audience, it was the "day of the sun"—Sunday. That was the day Christians gathered to celebrate the Paschal Mystery and carry out the remembrance, as Jesus had instructed them.

The Christians' year, too, assumed that Paschal shape. The first feast universally celebrated was Easter, which most Christians called *Pascha* or Passover. The Church added other feasts gradually until the year, by means of the days and seasons, told the story of the life of Christ. The festivals of the year mark the milestones of Jesus' life, from his conception through his birth, from his circumcision through his baptism, from his public life through his Passion, death, and Resurrection, from his ascension to his sending of the Holy Spirit at Pentecost.

These cycles of holy days are like a great curriculum of the Christian faith. It is through the feasts that believers begin to learn the dogmas. Christmas, with its carols and crèche, teaches the dogma of the Incarnation as powerfully as any theological treatise. The Easter liturgy, full of fire and water, shows us the new order of creation established by the risen Lord. Trinity Sunday gives us a day to sing with gusto about the most profound and mind-boggling doctrines.

The feasts of the saints teach us, too. They show us God's new creation in its glory: men and women fully alive in Christ. They show us the Christian vocation in all its variety as well, as we venerate the heroes of the faith from every land, every race, and every age. In a special way, we observe feasts in honor of the Blessed Virgin Mary, because God called her to be his mother and she remained faithful to her calling, occupying a unique place in salvation history and a lasting place in our hearts.

Just as the leaves change on the trees to mark time, so the Mass changes—subtly—throughout the year to reflect the different times and seasons.

The Scripture readings in the lectionary are keyed to the festivals and seasons. They reflect the events we celebrate. Some of the prayers change in a similar way. There are special versions to match the changing times and changing themes. Some of the Eucharistic Prayers allow for different insertions during the holy seasons.

During the seasons of Advent and Lent—which are seasons of penance and preparation—we suppress the jubilation of the *Gloria;* and during Lent we suppress the *Alleluia* as well. (We'll explain a bit more about these prayers, and the seasonal variations, in their particular chapters.)

The central events of our salvation take place in history, at specific times and in particular places. So we Christians have developed a highly refined way of marking the passage of time, keeping the life of Jesus Christ always before us. As we bring these mysteries to mind, we remember the marvels the Lord has done, but we "do this" in a way we learned from Jesus—a way that makes those marvels present for all time, so that the faithful can lay hold of them and be filled with saving grace.

TWO

THE MASS AS IT IS:
A CLOSER LOOK

The Procession

SOMETIMES, OUR CHURCHES ANNOUNCE THE approaching time of Mass by ringing chimes and bells, calling people to worship. The message of the bells is the ancient message of the Psalm: "Come, let us sing joyfully to the Lord. . . . Enter, let us bow down in worship; let us kneel before the Lord who made us. For this is our God, whose people we are" (Psalms 95:1, 6–7). Summoned, the people gather at *Church*—a word that in the Greek of the New Testament means not a building, but the *assembly* of God's people. It is the building that takes its name from the congregation, and not the other way around.

Before the Mass can begin, the priest must put on his vestments and make his entrance. Thus, the *procession,* the entry of the priest and others, may seem like a merely mechanical event: it moves necessary personnel in an orderly way along a prescribed route, from Point A (the sacristy) to Point B (the sanctuary).

But the procession is part of the ritual, and so it is rich in meaning. It symbolizes our earthly pilgrimage toward

heaven. We are a pilgrim people, and we're making our way
through life to God. We do not travel alone. Like the tribes
we read about in the Bible, we move through life as a family, and that family is the Catholic Church.

When we gather as God's family for the Mass, the procession brings the ministers—perhaps the altar servers, lector, and even the choir—and then, finally, the priest into
the sanctuary. On their way to the sanctuary, they represent
us all. We can see ourselves, by the grace of the Mass, making progress on the way to heaven.

Sometimes the procession is very short, and sometimes
it's very long and dramatic. Sometimes it is accompanied

The procession at the start of the Mass symbolizes our earthly
pilgrimage toward heaven. © *Paul Fetters*

by a hymn or instrumental music, sometimes by a simple antiphon—a verse from Scripture.

At the head of the procession may be a *crucifer,* an altar server bearing a cross. This simple, common image reminds us that Jesus is our "leader to salvation . . . made perfect through suffering" (Hebrews 2:10).

And that's why we've come to the church at the beautiful sound of the bells. "Therefore, since we are surrounded by so great a cloud of witnesses, let us rid ourselves of every burden and sin that clings to us and persevere in running the race that lies before us while keeping our eyes fixed on Jesus, the leader and perfecter of faith. For the sake of the joy that lay before him he endured the cross" (Hebrews 12:1–2).

The procession moves, outwardly, at a dignified pace. Inwardly, however, and spiritually, we are hastening to heaven, behind the leader who goes before us: Jesus Christ, crucified, risen, and glorified.

The Sign of the Cross

THE LITURGY BEGINS WITH THE Church's most basic blessing, most fundamental prayer: the *Sign of the Cross.* It is both a gesture and a vocal prayer. Using our right hand, we trace the shape of the cross over our upper body: from forehead to chest, and then from our left shoulder to our right. As we do, the priest says: "In the name of the Father and of the Son and of the Holy Spirit," and the congregation replies: "Amen."

Pope Benedict XVI described this simple action as "a kind of synthesis of our faith." It's a summary of the core doctrines of Christianity. By our words, it proclaims the Trinity of persons in the Godhead: Father, Son, and Holy Spirit. At the same time, it acknowledges the oneness of God, because we bless ourselves in a singular "name."

The gesture itself traces the way God loved the human race, descending from heaven to heart and taking flesh, and then ascending to heaven, taking our glorified human nature with him. Thus we conclude at the right shoulder, just as Jesus concluded his journey "at the right hand of the Father" in heaven. By the form of the cross, we also acknowledge the means of our redemption: the cross of Calvary, whose sacrifice is made present for us in the Mass.

The Sign of the Cross takes no more than a few seconds, but it speaks volumes of truth and sounds the depths of theology.

The early Christians loved to trace the sign, and today we can only imagine its ancient significance. In the ancient world, the cross was an instrument of torture and shame, a

The liturgy begins with the Sign of the Cross. Though simple, it is a summary of the core doctrines of Christianity. © *Paul Fetters*

method of execution reserved for the most hated criminals. Yet those Christians, who had seen men so tortured, drew the sign over their body at every opportunity, and they considered it a blessing.

The Sign of the Cross was their reminder of the extent of Jesus' love. He was willing to undergo the most humiliating death *for our sake*. Again, Pope Benedict put it well. The Sign of the Cross, he said, "tells how much God loves us; it tells us that there is a love in this world that is stronger than death, stronger than our weaknesses and sins. The power of love is stronger than the evil which threatens us."

We have been redeemed through the events that happened on one cross two thousand years ago. It also reminds us of our baptism, when a cleric signed us and said, "I claim you for Christ." We should remember this, and we should rejoice. It is, after all, the beginning of a celebration.

The priest follows the sign with a simple greeting, drawn from Scripture. There are several options, including this one from Saint Paul, which again invokes God as the Blessed Trinity: "The grace of our Lord Jesus Christ, and the love of God, and the communion of the Holy Spirit be with you all" (see 2 Corinthians 13:14). Or he may say, simply, "The Lord be with you," to which the congregation responds, "And with your Spirit." When we make that response, we are acknowledging the role of the Holy Spirit in the Mass. We are addressing Jesus Christ, who is the true priest presiding over every Mass.

The priest may also speak briefly about the occasion for the gathering or about some theme in the Bible readings for the day.

Confession and Mercy:
The Penitential Rite

WHEN WE GO TO MASS, we take our place among God's people. We go because we have been called. Yet we know we have not always been faithful to our calling. We know that we have not always lived up to the teaching of Jesus Christ. "If we say, 'We are without sin,' " says Saint John, "we deceive ourselves, and the truth is not in us" (1 John 1:8–9).

Weakness and a tendency to sin have, unfortunately, been part of our human condition, ever since the sin of our first parents, Adam and Eve. Nevertheless, Saint John adds in the very next verse of Scripture, "If we acknowledge our sins, [God] is faithful and just and will forgive our sins and cleanse us from every wrongdoing."

And so we come before the altar, we come before the Church, we come before Christ in a penitential spirit, and we express our sorrow in the traditional prayers. In the pages of the Bible, so many people acknowledge their weakness with the words "Lord, have mercy" (see Matthew 17:15, and Matthew 20:31); and so we do the same.

The Church has used this simple prayer since ancient times, sometimes as part of a long litany of petitions at the beginning of Mass. Now, we pray, repeating after the priest: "Lord, have mercy . . . Christ, have mercy . . . Lord, have mercy." We address the three petitions to the three persons of the Blessed Trinity. Sometimes people refer to this prayer as the *Kyrie* (pronounced *KEE-ree-ay*); *Kyrie* is the Greek word for "Lord."

Jesus once told a story that illuminates this part of the Mass. "Two people went up to the temple area to pray," he said. "One was a Pharisee and the other was a tax collector. The Pharisee took up his position and spoke this prayer to himself, 'O God, I thank you that I am not like the rest of humanity—greedy, dishonest, adulterous—or even like this tax collector. I fast twice a week, and I pay tithes on my whole income.' But the tax collector stood off at a distance and would not even raise his eyes to heaven but beat his breast and prayed, 'O God, be merciful to me, a sinner.' I tell you, the latter went home justified, not the former; for everyone who exalts himself will be humbled, and the one who humbles himself will be exalted" (Luke 18:10–14).

The one Jesus praised was the one who recognized his own failings. Both men needed mercy. Only one asked for it. Can we doubt that we, too, need forgiveness before we enter the presence of the all-holy God?

The Penitential Rite gives us a chance to recognize our failings and ask God to cleanse us of all that might hold us back from the celebration of the Eucharist. Our faith teaches us that this action will indeed remove the stain of any sins we have committed that are not mortal sins. (Mortal sins require forgiveness through the Sacrament of Reconciliation. There, the Church exercises the power of the keys, granted by Jesus to his apostles [see Matthew 16:19 and 18:18]. If we have committed any grave sin, we must first go to sacramental confession before we may receive Holy Communion.)

During this part of the Mass, the congregation may also pray a longer prayer, called the *Confiteor* (a Latin word meaning "I confess"; pronounced *cone-FEE-tay-or*):

> I confess to almighty God and to you, my brothers and sisters, that I have greatly sinned in my thoughts and in my words, in what I have done and in what I have failed to do, through my fault, through my fault, through my most grievous fault; therefore I ask blessed Mary ever-Virgin, all the angels and saints, and you, my brothers and sisters, to pray for me to the Lord our God.

As you and I acknowledge our sins, we take full responsibility. I have sinned through "my fault"—not someone else's. In order to emphasize the point, we repeat the phrase and intensify it: "through my fault, through my fault, through my most grievous fault." The prayer gives us a brief summary of the ways we can go wrong—by sins of word or deed, omission or commission. We say we're sorry for all of them.

Moreover, we say we're sorry not just with a word, but with a deed as well, a gesture. Like the tax collector in the story Jesus told, we strike our breast as we make the three-fold acknowledgment of our fault. We hope to go home justified, as the tax collector did.

As Christians, we wish to do better, but we should not despair because of our failures. The Bible makes it clear that we are wounded by sin, and while we may often be tempted and fall, we need not stay down. Jesus gives us the grace to rise again with him to the life of virtue. The choice is ours. The wise Solomon said: "the just man falls seven times and rises again, but the wicked stumble to ruin" (Proverbs 24:16). Now is our chance to rise again, in the Penitential Rite.

Sometimes, the priest celebrating Mass may substitute a "rite of sprinkling" for some or all of the prayers. He will douse a brush, branch, or special instrument called an *aspergilium* with holy water and sprinkle it on the congregation. This recalls the waters of baptism, which save us and wash away our sins.

No matter which option the priest should choose, the effect is the same: we have repented. Like the prodigal son in the parable, we have made our move toward our Father God, who is hurrying now to meet us.

The priest concludes the rite by offering a prayer asking God to have mercy, forgive our sins, and bring us to ever-lasting life.

One last word on sin: It's important that we understand the difference between mortal and venial sin, and that our understanding matches the doctrine of the Church. Some actions that the popular media describe as "peccadilloes" are actually quite serious offenses against the commandments of God. We should study the Church's moral teaching as it is expressed in the Catechism of the Catholic Church or some other Church-approved adult catechism.

Glory to God in the Highest!

IN THE PENITENTIAL RITE WE take a hard look at our own fallen humanity. We see ourselves as we are, and so we come to see more clearly who God is, especially in relation to a fallen world. We are moved to rejoice in our salvation—what the Almighty has done for us—but we also want to praise God simply for being God. If in the Penitential Rite we acknowledge our lowliness, in the very next prayer, the *Gloria,* we praise God's greatness.

The *Gloria* celebrates the glory of God, who, for our sake, has taken flesh in Jesus Christ.

The Church takes the opening lines of this prayer from the angels' song at the birth of Jesus. "And suddenly there was a multitude of the heavenly host with the angel, praising God and saying: 'Glory to God in the highest and on earth peace to those on whom his favor rests' " (Luke 2:13–14). The *Gloria* was the first Christmas carol, and in Latin it remains the refrain in many seasonal standards: *Gloria in excelsis Deo!*

The *Gloria* is the preeminent example of a prayer of

praise. The Church calls such a prayer a *doxology*—from the Greek words meaning "a word of praise"—and you may sometimes hear the *Gloria* called the "Great Doxology" or the "Major Doxology." It is the great one because we use it in the Mass, and because we learned it from the voices of the angels.

The *Gloria* adds a touch of Christmas to our celebrations throughout the year. It celebrates that Jesus Christ is the Son of God become man for our salvation. And the early Christians thought it proper to sing the same song in the Mass; for it is there that we experience, firsthand, the mystery of the Incarnation. Listen to Saint John Chrysostom: "The wise men adored this body when it lay in the manger; they prostrated themselves before it in fear and trembling. Now you behold the same body that the wise men adored in the manger, lying upon the altar; you also know its power and saving effect."

That's ample reason to give glory, and the *Gloria* is a hymn that rises to the occasion. It is a hymn of enthusiasm, ecstasy, an outpouring of song like the Gospel canticles of Mary (Luke 1:46–55) and Zechariah (Luke 1:68–79), or those found in the heavenly visions of the Book of Revelation (19:6–8).

> *Glory to God in the highest,*
> *and on earth peace to people of good will.*
> *We praise you,*
> *we bless you,*
> *we adore you,*
> *we glorify you,*
> *we give you thanks for your great glory,*

Lord God, heavenly King,
O God, almighty Father.
Lord Jesus Christ, Only Begotten Son,
Lord God, Lamb of God, Son of the Father,
you take away the sins of the world,
have mercy on us;
you take away the sins of the world,
receive our prayer;
you are seated at the right hand of the Father,
have mercy on us.
For you alone are the Holy One,
you alone are the Lord,
you alone are the Most High,
Jesus Christ,
with the Holy Spirit,
in the glory of God the Father.
Amen.

After its angelic opening and effusion of praise, the *Gloria* proceeds with a litany of scriptural titles for God: heavenly King, almighty Father, Only Begotten, Lord, Lamb of God, Most High, Christ. Originally composed in Greek, the *Gloria* takes a form that the early Church referred to as "private psalms," prayers composed by faithful Christians after the style of the biblical psalms of King David.

According to the ancient chronicles of the Church of Rome, the *Gloria* has been part of the Church's public prayer since around A.D. 128, when it was added to the nighttime Mass at Christmas. It was then that Pope Saint Telesphorus decreed: "at the opening of the sacrifice the angelic hymn should be repeated—that is, 'Glory to God in the highest!' "

The Church uses the *Gloria* in Sunday Masses as a form of celebration, except during the seasons of Advent and Lent, when the liturgy is more subdued and penitential. It is also used during certain feasts and solemnities when they fall on weekdays.

In the parts of the Mass we have seen so far, the Blessed Trinity has been a consistent theme: invoked in the Sign of the Cross, and again in the greeting, and again in the threefold form of the *Kyrie*. The *Gloria* further develops this theme as it praises the persons of the Godhead in all their heavenly glory.

To glorify God is the hallmark of faith. So said Saint

During the opening prayer, or "collect," the priest emphasizes the special theme or themes of the Mass. © *Paul Fetters*

Paul as he praised the faith of Abraham (Romans 4:20). We can see this reflected through the ages in the lives of the saints. Saint John Chrysostom lived by the motto "Glory to God for all things," and he died with those words on his lips. Saint Ignatius Loyola wished his every action, and the actions of all his followers, the Jesuits, to rise "to the greater glory of God."

So our song rises at Sunday Mass.

After the *Gloria* and a brief moment of silence, the priest offers an "opening prayer," sometimes called a "collect," that emphasizes some special theme or themes of the Mass. The congregation takes this prayer as its own by responding, "Amen."

The First Reading

FROM THE *GLORIA* AND OPENING prayer, we proceed to a series of readings from the Bible, passages the Church has excerpted and arranged for the Mass in a meaningful way. We have arrived at the *Liturgy of the Word*.

"Faith comes from what is heard," Saint Paul said (Romans 10:17). And so we receive the words of the Bible as the earliest Christians received them. We receive them from the Church. Remember that, for many centuries, there were no printing presses; books were very costly; and many people could not read. Still, Christians received the Scriptures in an orderly fashion as they attended Mass, week after week, year after year (and sometimes day after day), throughout their lives. In fact, the early Church defined its Scriptures as those books that could legitimately be read during the Mass—for no other documents, no other words may be proclaimed as "the Word" at Mass.

The Church sets out a thorough program of readings in a book called the *lectionary*. On most Sundays, these begin with a selection from the Old Testament.

The Old Testament is what we call the forty-six books that make up the first (and larger) portion of the Bible. These books record the history of salvation from the moment of creation till the coming of Jesus Christ. (Salvation history from that moment forward is the subject of the New Testament, the second part of the Bible.) The Old Testament includes the Pentateuch (the first five books) as well as books of history, wisdom that is a little like philosophy, and prophecy.

What we call the Old Testament, Jesus and the apostles simply called "the Scriptures." The Old Testament books were the Church's first Scriptures—and they remain our first Scriptures, in order of sequence, whenever we go to Mass. Jesus himself proclaimed the Old Testament to have an abiding value: "Do not think that I have come to abolish the law or the prophets. I have come not to abolish but to fulfill. Amen, I say to you, until heaven and earth pass away, not the smallest letter or the smallest part of a letter will pass from the law" (Matthew 5:17–18).

Christianity is unintelligible apart from the religion of ancient Israel—God's primordial covenant with his chosen people. Jesus understood himself and explained himself in light of the Old Testament: "Then beginning with Moses and all the prophets, [Jesus] interpreted to them what referred to him in all the scriptures" (Luke 24:27). Following his master, Saint Paul taught the Church that the Israelites "were entrusted with the utterances of God" (Romans 3:2). Thus, Christians have always venerated the Scriptures of ancient Israel.

The books of the Old Testament are, as we proclaim in the Mass: "The Word of the Lord." They are God's inspired Word. They are a Word he spoke through human authors, who freely cooperated with his action.

Catholics believe that *all the Old Testament books*—though they vary in style, genre, and content, and though they were written over the span of a millennium and more—have a single common subject, and that is Jesus Christ. This is how a third-century Bible scholar, an Egyptian named Origen, explained it: "Christ, the Word of God, was in Moses and the Prophets. . . . Moses or the Prophets said and did everything they did because they were filled with the Spirit of Christ."

God revealed the Old Testament as a preparation for the New Testament. The Old prophesies—that is, it foreshadows, foretells, prefigures—the New. The Old contains the New, though in a hidden way. As Jesus himself said, he came to "fulfill" the law and the prophets. In the New Testament, that fulfillment is complete. No longer hidden, the Word is made flesh and dwelling among us.

Thus, we can fully understand the Old Testament only when we see it through the lens of the Gospel. It is like a mystery story whose details are comprehensible only in light of the story's ending. But God, the consummate Author, had left us clues at every stage of the story's development.

In the Liturgy of the Word, the first reading, like all the readings, is read aloud from a special lectern called the *ambo*.

You'll notice that brief periods of silence come at intervals during the Liturgy of the Word. There is silence be-tween the readings and the Responsorial Psalm, between the second reading and the Gospel, and after the homily. These are important moments for meditation, when we re-ceive of the Word of God into our hearts.

The Responsorial Psalm

BETWEEN THE FIRST READING AND the second, we actually have another "reading" from the Bible. This one, however, is participatory. It's a reading shared by a leader—either
a lector or a cantor—and the entire congregation.

The Responsorial Psalm is usually taken from the biblical Book of Psalms, the great collection of the hymns and
prayerful poems of ancient Israel. (It is likely that many of
the Psalms were used in the ancient liturgies of the Jerusalem Temple.) On rare occasions, the lectionary presents
another biblical canticle. Mary's *Magnificat* (Luke 1:46–55),
for example, is sometimes used on feasts dedicated to her
honor.

Most of the time, however, we pray the Psalms, and we
do so in a call-and-response fashion. The lector reads a series of lines—or the cantor sings them—and the congregation responds with an *antiphon,* a line repeated at intervals.

It is interesting to note that antiphonal singing has been
part of the Mass since the very beginnings of Christianity.
It is probably something we learned from ancient Judaism.

In A.D. 111, a Roman governor named Pliny observed that the Christians in his region met on Sunday "before dawn and sing responsively a hymn" before partaking of "ordinary and innocent food." An early tradition records that Saint Ignatius of Antioch, a contemporary of the apostles, introduced antiphonal singing into the Church after he had a vision of the angels singing that way in heaven.

When we pray the Psalms this way, we are praying as Jesus did, as Mary did, and as the apostles did. The Psalms of Israel came easily to their mind in all circumstances. The Book of Psalms is the Old Testament book most often quoted in the New Testament.

It's easy to see why the Psalms were so memorable. Poetry makes things easier to remember. Melody makes poetry more memorable still. The lines of the Psalms stick with us: "Taste and see the goodness of the Lord" . . . "The Lord is my shepherd. There is nothing I shall want" . . . "I rejoiced when I heard them say, 'Let us go to the house of the Lord' " . . . "This is the day the Lord has made. Let us rejoice and be glad."

One of the Church fathers, Saint Basil the Great, told his priests that the Psalms were useful precisely *because* they were remembered. People might forget the homily, even if the priest is very well prepared, but they'll remember the antiphon of the Psalm, because it's melodic, and they'll sing it often through the day.

Another Church father, Saint Athanasius, noted that the Psalms contained "all things human"—joy, gratitude, repentance, cries for help, pleas for justice, and appeals for mercy. Noting the Church's Christ-centered reading of all Scripture, Saint Augustine taught that the Psalms represent the prayer *of* Christ, prayer *about* Christ, and prayer *to* Christ.

Saint Jerome exhorted his flock not to be shy about singing: "Even if you're tone-deaf, to use a vulgar phrase, if your works are good, your song is sweet to God. If you would serve Christ, don't worry about your voice, but concentrate on the good words you sing."

So let your voice be heard at the Responsorial Psalm. Let it join the voices of the others around you. If you do, you'll find that the ancient songs rise as readily to your lips and your mind as they did for Jesus and his first disciples. The Psalms are something that go home with Christians, when Christians go home from Mass. Indeed, they go with us wherever we go. Saint John Chrysostom said: "Are you a craftsman? As you sit at work, sing Psalms . . . You shall be able to sit in your workshop as in a monastery."

The Second Reading

AT MASS ON SUNDAYS, AS well as special memorials and feast days, the Church prescribes a second Scripture reading before the proclamation of the Gospel. This reading is usually chosen from the New Testament books that are not "Gospels"—the letters of the apostles, the Acts, and the visionary Book of Revelation.

The form of these books is especially well suited for the Mass. Indeed, many of them were written precisely for that purpose: to be read at Mass. At the close of one letter, Saint Paul said: "I adjure you by the Lord that this letter be read to all the brothers" (1 Thessalonians 5:27). The Book of Revelation begins with the benediction: "Blessed is the one who reads aloud and blessed are those who listen to this prophetic message" (Revelation 1:3).

So, still today, we read aloud and we listen. In the second reading we often catch glimpses of the problems and the progress of the Church's first generation. They struggled to be faithful to the Gospel amid a sometimes-hostile pagan culture. They knew the pain of estrangement from family members and friends who misunderstood them. They disagreed with one another about practical matters, even related to the Church. They rejoiced at the conversion of friends who were sinners. They mourned when fellow Christians went backsliding into immorality. They loved the Mass, too, as we do (listen closely to 1 Corinthians, chapters 10 and 11).

From the second reading, we come to know that our fellowship is not just with Christians in our parish, or in our time. It is *catholic*—that is, universal. It embraces all people of the world, at every period of the Church's history. We are still living in the Church described in the apostles' letters. We want to be faithful, as that first generation was, even if we should undergo persecution.

We are dependent upon the witness of these ancestors in the faith. And so, when the lector announces the second reading as "The Word of the Lord," we respond with grateful voices: "Thanks be to God!"

Alleluia!

ALLELUIA IS ONE OF TWO Hebrew words that have endured, untranslated, for use in the Mass. (The other is *Amen.*)

Alleluia (sometimes spelled *Hallelujah*) means "Praise the Lord." That is what we do when we rise to hear the proclamation of the Gospel.

Praise is the purest form of prayer, because it seeks nothing for itself, but only God's glory. We *ask* God for good things. We *thank* God for graces we have received. Our gratitude, however, moves us to consider not just what God has done for us, but *who God is*. And so we praise the Lord.

The Hebrew word *Hallelujah* has, since ancient times, been an important part of the Passover celebration of the Jews. It is a key word in certain Psalms, called *Hallel* or "Praise" Psalms. In the time of Jesus, when the Jerusalem Temple was still standing, the assisting priests (the Levites) would chant a group of these Psalms (113–118) continuously during the sacrifice of the Passover lambs. Families would chant two of these Psalms (113–114) during the Passover meal at home. This was likely the "hymn" that Jesus and his disciples sang at the end of the Last Supper (see Matthew 26:30 and Mark 14:26).

Thus, this classic expression of praise—*Alleluia!*—has always been integral to the Passover, and so it became an important part of the Christian celebration of the Paschal Mystery.

Consider the reasons devout Jews have given for their praise. In the Talmud (from around A.D. 200) we can find the oldest account of the rites of the Passover meal: "In every generation a man must so regard himself as if he came forth himself out of Egypt . . . He brought us out from bondage to freedom, from sorrow to gladness, and from mourning to a festival day, and from darkness to great light, and from servitude to redemption; so let us say before him the *Hallelujah*."

This is what Jesus was celebrating with his closest friends at the Last Supper. It is what he continues to celebrate with us at every Mass. Now he delivers us—from bondage to freedom, sorrow to gladness, mourning to joy, darkness to light, slavery to redemption. This is the meaning of our salvation. This is the gift we have received with the Gospel. And so when we stand to receive the Gospel, we raise our own great *Hallel*. We say or sing *Alleluia*.

The Book of Revelation depicts heavenly worship as the "Marriage Supper of the Lamb," replete with many Passover images and prayers. Chapter 19 shows heaven and earth chanting praise irrepressibly—with four *Hallelujahs* in just six verses. It is a great festival of praise, and so is our experience of the Mass.

After this I heard what sounded like the loud voice of a great multitude in heaven, saying: "Alleluia! Salvation, glory, and might belong to our God" . . . A voice coming from the throne said: "Praise our God, all you his servants, [and] you who revere him, small and great." Then I heard something like the sound of a great multitude or the sound of rushing water or mighty peals of thunder, as they said: "Alleluia! The Lord has established his reign, [our] God, the almighty" (Revelation 19:1, 5–6).

The Church omits the *Alleluia* during the season of Lent, for reasons that should be obvious. During Lent, we cultivate a longing to celebrate the Passover of Jesus Christ, his Paschal Mystery: his Easter. As we wait, we look forward to the time of the *Hallel,* the season of *Alleluia.* At Easter Vigil, we restore the *Alleluia,* and the churches ring out with praise at the good news.

The Gospel

FOR THE FIRST TWO READINGS and the Psalm, we have been seated, to signify our receptiveness to God's Word. Now, however, we stand to recognize the arrival of the great King, Jesus, in the words of the Gospel.

The priest or deacon precedes his reading of the Gospel by repeating a portion of the introductory rites: "The Lord be with you," to which everyone now responds: "And with your Spirit." It is as if we are beginning again, drawing still nearer to Christ, whom we acknowledge as present in his inspired Word. For, as the Church declares in its General Instruction of the Roman Missal: "When the Sacred Scriptures are read in the Church, God himself speaks to his people, and Christ, present in his own word, proclaims the Gospel."

The word *gospel* means, literally, "good news" or "glad tidings." It is the word the apostles used to describe their proclamation of Jesus' saving work (see Romans 1:1, 1:15).

The Gospel readings at Mass are chosen from the first four books of the New Testament, the accounts of Jesus' earthly ministry. The priest announces the source of his selection as he says, "A reading from the holy Gospel according to Saint Matthew" (or Mark or Luke or John). The congregation responds by saying, "Glory to you, O Lord," and making a small Sign of the Cross over the forehead, the lips, and the breast. The priest prays quietly a prayer that illuminates our simple gesture. He prays that the Lord may be in his heart and on his lips, and make him worthy to proclaim the Gospel.

The Sunday readings unfold over a three-year cycle of Gospel readings. The first year, Year A, uses the Gospel According to Saint Matthew. Year B follows Saint Mark. Year C follows Saint Luke. Saint John's Gospel is used often in the Church's special seasons, and it also fills out Year B, since Saint Mark's Gospel is relatively brief.

Often on Sundays the Gospel echoes themes that have been introduced in the first reading, and sometimes in the Responsorial Psalm as well. The Church's lectionary arranges passages to show how the content of the Bible is united. It is one story, with one principal author: God himself, who inspired the human authors. The characters, laws, and events of the Old Testament foreshadow and find fulfillment in the life and grace of Jesus Christ.

The lectionary is a great blessing. It is a teacher. It is a treasure chest. It ensures that faithful Catholics hear the Bible in its fullness, and not just a few favorite portions chosen according to the interests or idiosyncrasies of one or another preacher. It places the Bible front and center as the Church's book—and the Gospel front and center as the heart of the Bible.

The lectionary presents all the readings together on the page. Some parishes, however, keep a separate Book of the Gospels—an ornate book, beautifully bound, sometimes encased in precious metals. This, too, is an outward sign of the Gospels' value in the Church. They are a holy book— *the* Holy Book. If all the Bible is a temple, then the Gospels are the Holy of Holies. Bound together, they are treated as a sacred object. The priest, in fact, shows his affection and reverence for the sacred page by kissing it, a very ancient custom.

Only a priest, bishop, or deacon may read the Gospel at Mass. They receive this authority with the sacrament of Holy Orders. (During Holy Week, however, lay readers may assume certain roles in the reading of the long Passion narratives.)

By the way we treat the Gospel, we acknowledge that it is the high point of the Liturgy of the Word. In the way it is proclaimed—and sometimes in the way it is printed in a book—the Gospel is something set apart, and that is the very definition of holiness.

At the end of the reading, the priest reminds everyone that we have heard "The Gospel of the Lord." And the congregation responds, directly to Jesus, who is present: "Praise to you, Lord Jesus Christ."

The Homily

FOLLOWING THE GOSPEL, WE COME to the homily. In the homily, a member of the clergy—a priest, deacon, or bishop—explains a passage of Scripture and gives practical applications.

The homily is a graced moment to share the faith. Christian friends may encourage us, correct us, and cajole us in many circumstances. But the context of the Mass—the remembrance of Christ and his real presence—makes the homily a preeminent place for us to hear what we need to hear. In the homily, we learn and grow with help not only from the preacher, but from the Holy Spirit. It's the clear teaching of the Church that "the liturgical homily" holds "pride of place" among "all forms of Christian instruction" (see CCC, n. 132).

The great, living, apostolic tradition is ours to pass on to a generation that longs to be part of something good, life-giving, and meaningful. So the Church shares the faith in the spirit of the first Christians, who gathered to receive the apostles' teaching in the context of "the breaking of the bread and the prayers" (Acts 2:42). The Church does so in the spirit of Jesus, who addressed synagogue gatherings (see Luke 4:16–20) and, on the day of his Resurrection, with the disciples at Emmaus, "interpreted to them what referred to him in all the Scriptures" (Luke 24:27).

The apostles followed this pattern wherever they went. Later in the Acts of the Apostles (20:11), we find Saint Paul preaching to the Church's assembly throughout the night, "until daybreak"!

Homilies today tend not to run on so long—but they are no less an important part of the Mass. Since so much in our culture changes so rapidly, it is essential that the teaching of Christ be applied to circumstances of our day in a way that allows the believer to see the full implications of the profession of faith. Catholic faith is not merely about abstract points of theology. Nor is it something we dust off and wear

During the homily, a priest, deacon, or bishop explains a passage of Scripture and gives practical applications. © *Paul Fetters*

for an hour on Sunday. It is a commitment of our whole life, and the homily shows how the faith applies to life—at home, at work, at leisure. As Saint Justin Martyr put it in A.D. 155: "When the reader has finished, he who presides over those gathered admonishes and challenges them to imitate these beautiful things."

By explaining the Scriptures, "the homily, as an integral part of the liturgy, increases the Word's effectiveness." (So we read in the Church's General Instruction of the Roman Missal.)

How does the preacher do that? The ways are as many and as varied as the personalities and interests of the preacher. One preacher may have a mastery of a wide variety of styles and approaches. The Church's preachers learn from Jesus, whose sermons proceed by use of stories, analogies, commands, even confrontation. So it remains today: a homily can take many different forms. There was a time when moralizing dominated homilies. Today, the challenge the priest faces is to use the homily not only to encourage his flock in the practice of the faith, but also to share with them the faith itself, the very content—the life-giving reality—of God's Word.

Today's preacher may also draw from a wealth of resources. The three-year cycle the lectionary provides may be richly integrated with the Catechism of the Catholic Church to touch on every aspect of our faith in a way that roots it in Scripture and relates it to daily life. Pope Benedict XVI laid out a clear plan for such teaching in his letter *Sacramentum Caritatis:* "The catechetical . . . aim of the homily should not be forgotten. During the course of the liturgical year it is appropriate to offer the faithful, prudently and on the basis of the three-year lectionary, 'thematic' homilies treating the great themes of the Christian faith, on the basis of what has been authoritatively proposed by the Magisterium in the four 'pillars' of the Catechism of the Catholic Church . . . , namely: the profession of faith, the celebration of the Christian mystery, life in Christ and Christian prayer."

Still, the effect of the homily is not so much the work of the preacher as it is a work of the Spirit. So we may sometimes draw tremendous insights from a homily that was hastily prepared when Father was pressed for time because of all his parish duties, or when he was having a bad day. It's not about flash and dazzle. It's about our attentiveness to hear that "tiny whispering sound" (1 Kings 19:12) that is the voice of God, speaking to our hearts, speaking through the ministry of others.

You may sometimes notice parishioners making the Sign of the Cross at the beginning or the end of the homily. This is a good, practical way of calling upon God's help, to make the Word "actual"—to make the Word reside in our hearts.

At Emmaus, Jesus moved his gathering from the Word to the sacrament. After he opened up the Scriptures for the disciples, he made himself known to them "in the breaking of the bread." As the Liturgy of the Word begins to draw to a close, the homily points in the direction of the rite we are about to celebrate: the Liturgy of the Eucharist.

The Profession of Faith

THE MEMBERS OF THE CONGREGATION now stand up and, together, proclaim their common faith.

When we recite the *creed* at Mass, we act in communion with each other and with the whole body of Christ—the Church throughout the world and down through the ages, the saints of the past as well as our current neighbors. No Catholic is an island. No Catholic lives alone in the faith. Even someone who lives on a desert island, even someone who languishes in solitary confinement, if they keep the faith, they live in Christ with the whole Church. And that's why we stand and make our profession together, as a community—as a communion.

The English word *creed* comes from the first word of the ancient Roman baptismal profession as it is rendered in Latin: *credo,* which means "I believe."

We recite the creed as a summary of our faith. We publicly acknowledge that what we have heard is the Word of God—what has been proclaimed in the readings and in all our upbringing in the faith. And we publicly announce our adherence to the teaching of Christ—everything we have received in tradition from the apostles.

We believe in God. We believe in Christ. We believe in the Holy Spirit. And we believe in Christ's Church, the Catholic Church. These are the four great proclamations of the creed that we recite on Sundays.

Christians have always used creedal statements—brief summaries of the faith—as part of their sacramental worship. It is a way of affirming the faith before consummating that faith in Holy Communion. In the New Testament we find short formulas that summarize key doctrines: for example, "Jesus is Lord!" (Romans 10:9, 1 Corinthians 12:3). In those early days, that doctrine—Jesus' divinity—would have been the most difficult for non-Christians to accept. To recite the creed was to set oneself apart, to commit oneself to a distinctive way of thinking and living.

These simple statements gradually developed into longer sequences of "articles," lines affirming doctrines distinctive to the Christian faith. These early summaries were called the "rule of faith," and they found final form as the early baptismal creeds, such as the Apostles' Creed—a relatively brief statement, which is still used, especially during Lent and Easter time and in Masses for children.

The creed we usually recite today is commonly called the Nicene Creed, after the fourth-century Council of Nicaea, which produced its basic articles. The creed is more accurately called the Nicene-Constantinopolitan Creed, because it was more fully developed at the Council of Constantinople, later in the fourth century. At these councils (held in lands that are now part of Turkey), the Church made a definitive response to heresies that threatened to confuse believers and divide God's family. At Nicaea (A.D. 325), the Church opposed those who denied the divinity of Jesus Christ. At Constantinople, the Church condemned a heresy that denied the divinity of the Holy Spirit.

The Church developed its creeds slowly, deliberately, over the course of centuries. Every word was chosen carefully, tested, contested, debated, and only then confirmed. Christians shed their blood and died in defense of subtle shades of meaning in the words chosen for the creeds.

Within every article is an essential doctrine of the faith—a dogma that must be accepted if we are to claim the name Christian. Behind most articles lurks some dark challenge to the faith. For example, against ancient heretics who rejected the heritage of Judaism, the Church required Christians to affirm that the Holy Spirit "has spoken through the prophets." Against those who rejected Jesus' humanity, we proclaim that he "was incarnate"—that is, he took on flesh—"and became man" and "suffered death and was buried."

The Church gives us the creed so that we can prepare ourselves to celebrate the Eucharist. In the creed we declare our unity with Christ and the Church. In the Eucharist we consummate that unity. What we accept verbally in the creed, we accomplish bodily in Holy Communion.

Recently, the phrasing of our translation was changed to make it reflect the historical creeds with greater accuracy. Some of the terms—like "consubstantial" and "incarnate"—are taken from the unfamiliar and technical language of theology. But no other words describe the mysteries with such precision. The Father and the Son are *of the same substance*. The Word *took flesh*—became incarnate.

Through repeated, prayerful profession over the course of a lifetime, we make such words our own, and we make the faith our own.

> *I believe in one God,*
> *the Father almighty,*
> *maker of heaven and earth,*
> *of all things visible and invisible.*
>
> *And in one Lord Jesus Christ,*
> *the Only Begotten Son of God,*
> *born of the Father before all ages.*
> *God from God, Light from Light,*
> *true God from true God,*
> *begotten, not made, consubstantial with the Father;*
> *through him all things were made.*
> *For us men and for our salvation*
> *he came down from heaven,*

[From the start of the following line till the word "man," we bow our heads to show our reverence for Jesus.]

> *and by the Holy Spirit was incarnate*
> *of the Virgin Mary,*
> *and became man.*
> *For our sake he was crucified under Pontius Pilate,*
> *he suffered death and was buried,*
> *and rose again on the third day*
> *in accordance with the Scriptures.*
> *He ascended into heaven*
> *and is seated at the right hand of the Father.*

He will come again in glory
to judge the living and the dead
and his kingdom will have no end.

And in the Holy Spirit, the Lord, the giver of life,
who proceeds from the Father and the Son,
who with the Father and the Son is adored and glorified,
who has spoken through the prophets.
And one, holy, catholic and apostolic Church.
I confess one baptism for the forgiveness of sins
and I look forward to the resurrection of the dead
and the life of the world to come. Amen.

Prayer of the Faithful

A RECURRING THEME IN THE New Testament letters is the apostles' concern for proper conduct at worship—at Mass. This is a special concern in the First Letter to Timothy, where we read: "First of all, then, I ask that supplications, prayers, petitions, and thanksgivings [in Greek, *eucharistias*] be offered for everyone, for kings and for all in authority, that we may lead a quiet and tranquil life in all devotion and dignity. This is good and pleasing to God our savior" (1 Timothy 2:1–3).

In the general intercessions of the Mass—also called the "petitions" or "prayers of the faithful"—we seek to fulfill the apostles' request and please God our savior, who himself urged us: "Ask and it will be given to you; seek and you will find; knock and the door will be opened to you" (Matthew 7:7).

In baptism, each and every Christian receives a share in Christ's priesthood (see Revelation 1:6 and 1 Peter 2:9). Living in Christ, every Christian stands as a mediator between God and the world, offering "supplications, prayers,

petitions . . . for everyone." Since our most powerful prayer
is the Holy Mass, we use the occasion to raise our prayer on
behalf of ourselves and others. When we do so, the Church
says in its General Instruction of the Roman Missal, we are
"exercising our priestly function."

The priest who is celebrating Mass introduces the prayer,
usually while standing at the presider's chair. At the ambo,
a deacon or layperson announces the intentions, which may
vary from week to week, taking into consideration the current concerns of the community. Each petition ends with an
invitation for the assembly to join in the prayer: for example, "Let us pray to the Lord." And the assembly, in unison,
gives some customary response: for example, "Lord, hear
our prayer."

The Roman Missal indicates that the sequence of intentions should follow this general outline:

a. for the needs of the Church;

b. for public authorities and the salvation of the
    whole world;

c. for those oppressed by any need;

d. for the local community.

In particular celebrations, such as weddings or funerals,
the series of intercessions may refer more specifically to the
occasion.

This is another part of the Mass that Saint Justin Martyr
illuminated back in the second century: "Then we all rise

together and offer prayers for ourselves—and for all others, wherever they may be."

Just a few years after Saint Justin, a North African theologian named Tertullian described the petitions at Mass, playfully, as a sort of "wrestling" with God: "We meet together as an assembly and congregation so that, as we are united in offering our prayer to God, we may wrestle with him in our supplications. God delights in this violence. We pray, too, for the emperors, for their ministers and for all in authority, for the welfare of the world, for the prevalence of peace, for the delay of the final consummation." So we see the prayers had not changed much in the century and a half since Saint Paul's day. Nor have they changed much in the two thousand years since then.

Tertullian went on, in another book, to note that our prayer has the power to accomplish many things: "to transform the weak, to restore the sick, to purge the possessed, to open prison bars, to loose the bonds of the innocent. Likewise it washes away faults, repels temptations, extinguishes persecutions, consoles the faint-hearted, cheers the high-spirited, escorts travelers, appeases waves, makes robbers stand aghast, nourishes the poor, governs the rich, upraises the fallen, arrests the falling, confirms the standing. Prayer is the wall of faith: her arms and missiles against the foe who keeps watch over us on all sides."

Does this mean that God will always give us all that we want, exactly as we want it, just because we prayed for it at Mass? No, of course not. God is our Father, and no parent would do that. God will, however, always give us what we need. Tertullian explained that our prayer does not eliminate suffering, but rather "it supplies the suffering, and the feeling, and the grieving, with endurance; it amplifies grace by virtue, that faith may know what she obtains from the Lord, understanding what—for God's name's sake—she suffers."

Saint Paul earnestly prayed for relief from his own suffering, but God said to him, "My grace is sufficient for you, for power is made perfect in weakness" (2 Corinthians 12:9). God's grace will be enough for us, too. Thus, while we ask for relief of the world's ills, we ask also for the grace to endure them, if that is what God wants from us.

For we know from experience that suffering is a school of wisdom and kindness. Many of the wisest and kindest people we know are those who have suffered most. Christ himself showed us that the way to glory passes through great suffering and even death. Yet he also showed us the necessity of constant prayer. He prayed without ceasing and calls us to do the same.

So with every Mass we raise our prayers. Like Saint Paul, we offer our prayers, petitions, and Eucharist (*eucharistias*) for everyone, and we do this explicitly and specifically in the Prayer of the Faithful.

The Offertory

NOW BEGINS THE SECOND "HALF" of the Mass: the Liturgy
of the Eucharist. It is known also as the "Mass of the Faithful," because in ancient times only the baptized were allowed
to stay at Mass for this portion. Nor could any Christian stay
who had arrived with an unforgiven mortal sin.

Now begins the sacrificial portion of the Mass: the offering, the remembrance that Jesus asked of his apostles at
the Last Supper. The sacrifice starts with an offering, and
that's why this moment is called the offertory.

We begin by bringing our gifts to the altar. That's a very
general way of describing what happens, but it's accurate.
We bring our gifts—material gifts and spiritual gifts. We
bring what we have and what we are, and we acknowledge
that it all comes from God and it all belongs to God.

Since the earliest days of the Church, Christians have
used this time to "take up a collection" or "pass the basket."
Today we collect money that is used for the upkeep of the
Church and the funding of charitable activities. In the first
centuries, Christians would bring whatever they had and

place it by the altar, leaving it at the disposal of the priest or the local bishop. Saint Hippolytus wrote of the contributions left at the altar in third-century Rome: grapes, figs, pomegranates, olives, pears, apples, blackberries, peaches, cherries, almonds, and plums—and sometimes flowers, especially roses and lilies.

Here is Tertullian's description of a second-century African collection and distribution:

Everyone puts in a small donation, but only if they want to, and only if they are able: for there is no compulsion; all is voluntary. These gifts are like piety's deposit fund. For they are not taken from there and spent

During the offertory, members of the congregation bring to the altar the bread and wine that will be offered in the Eucharist. © *Paul Fetters*

on parties, drinking binges, and restaurants, but to support and bury poor people, to supply the wants of orphan boys and girls who have no possessions, and of homebound old people; and those who have suffered shipwreck; and if there happen to be any in the mines, or banished to the islands, or shut up in the prisons, for nothing but their fidelity to the cause of God's Church. They become the nurslings of their confession.

Such charity has always been the mark of Christianity, setting it apart, in the ancient world, from pagan philanthropy. In the pagan world, wealthy people were expected to placate the poor for the sake of the social order; and many rich people gave money to earn fame or immortality. But Christians gave for God's sake. Saint Paul records this abundantly as he travels (see Romans 15:26 and 1 Corinthians 16:1–2). Why did Christians give so generously? Paul explained: "Through the evidence of this service, you are glorifying God for your obedient confession of the Gospel of Christ and the generosity of your contribution to them and to all others" (2 Corinthians 9:13).

Sometimes, selected members of the congregation will bring the collection to the altar, along with the bread and wine to be offered in the Eucharist.

Over time, it became necessary to limit the gifts that should be brought to the altar during the offertory. The Church wanted people to distinguish the essential elements—which are those that Jesus offered, the bread and the wine—from all other gifts we wish to give to Christ and to charity.

Still, the gifts we bring to the altar stand not just for

themselves, but for all creation—and for *our* very selves. Through the *kingship* we share with Christ, we have dominion over the earth. We are stewards of the produce of the earth, which now we bring to the altar. Through the *priesthood* we share with Christ, we offer the earth and everything in it in sacrifice to God our heavenly Father.

The Preparation of the Gifts

WHILE THE CONGREGATION TAKES UP the collection, the priest (or if present, the deacon) prepares the altar. He places the cloths, the corporal and the purificator. He positions the missal, paten, and chalice.

What follows then is a series of prayers, ritual actions, and exchanges between the priest and the congregation. They're rich in meaning and symbolism. Let's just proceed through them first, watching as we go, and then we'll go back and examine them more closely.

The priest lifts up the paten that holds the bread, and he praises God: "Blessed are you, Lord God of all creation, for through your goodness we have received the bread we offer you: fruit of the earth and work of human hands, it will become for us the bread of life." The congregation responds: "Blessed be God for ever."

He then pours wine and a little bit of water into the chalice as he prays: "By the mystery of this water and wine may we come to share in the divinity of Christ who humbled himself to share in our humanity."

Father then elevates the chalice and pronounces a similar blessing: "Blessed are you, Lord God of all creation, for through your goodness we have received the wine we offer you: fruit of the vine and work of human hands, it will become our spiritual drink."

The priest then prays quietly over the chalice: "With humble spirit and contrite heart may we be accepted by you, O Lord, and may our sacrifice in your sight this day be pleasing to you, Lord God."

If there are altar servers at Mass, they will be standing ready at the side of the altar, with a pitcher of water, a small bowl or basin (the *lavabo*), and a towel. The priest washes his hands as he quietly prays: "Wash me, O Lord, from my iniquity and cleanse me from my sin."

Finally, turning to face the congregation, he extends and then joins his hands, saying: "Pray, brethren [or 'brothers

After preparing the altar, the priest lifts the paten with the bread and praises God. © *Paul Fetters*

and sisters'], that my sacrifice and yours may be acceptable to God, the almighty Father."

The people stand up and reply: "May the Lord accept the sacrifice at your hands for the praise and glory of his name, for our good and the good of all his holy Church."

So many historical and spiritual currents converge in this brief passage. When the priest pronounces the two blessings—the "blessing over bread" and "blessing over wine"—he is quite likely doing what Jesus did at the Last Supper. For the Passover meal includes those two actions accompanied by familiar words: "Blessed are you, Lord our God, king of the universe, who creates the fruit of the earth . . . Blessed are you, Lord our God, king of the universe, creator of the fruit of the vine." Archaeologists have

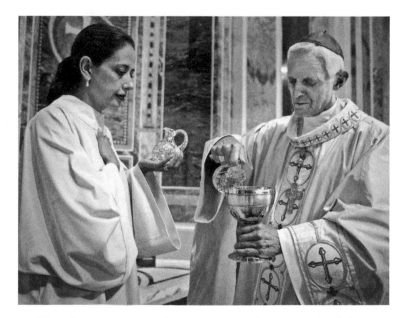

The priest pours wine and a small amount of water into the chalice, then elevates the chalice. © *Paul Fetters*

found these blessings among the ruins of synagogues from the first millennium.

Why does the priest mix a little bit of water with the wine? There is a practical, historical reason, and several symbolic interpretations. The historical fact is that that was the custom for most Mediterranean people living in the time of Jesus Christ. They stored wine in a concentrated form, and then diluted it at mealtime. Most of the ancient descriptions of the Passover meal describe the mixing of water with wine.

The Church, however, insisted on retaining this gesture long after the customs of wine storage had changed.

Altar servers assist the priest in washing his hands. © *Paul Fetters*

As a symbol, it had staying power. First of all, it provided a historical connection with the Passover *seder* meal, which Christians were eager to preserve. But there's still more. In the second century, Saint Irenaeus of Lyon, in France, saw that mixture as a symbol of the union of the human and divine natures in Jesus Christ: like the water and wine, they were so close as to be inseparable. Some decades later, Saint Cyprian, a North African, saw the mixture as a symbol of the communion of Christ with the Church—again, so close as to be indistinguishable from one another. And, of course, down the centuries, many saints have seen the mixture of wine and water as a vivid image of the blood and water that poured forth from the pierced side of Christ on the cross (see John 19:34).

As the priest elevates the gifts, he evokes many figures from the Bible. He reminds us of Melchizedek, the first person to be called a priest in the pages of Scripture. As Melchizedek lifts his offering of bread and wine, he says: "Blessed be Abram by God Most High, creator of heaven and earth; and blessed be God Most High" (Genesis 14:19–20).

The priest also stands at the altar as the priests of the Jerusalem Temple stood at their altar of sacrifice, in the time of Jesus and many centuries before. Like those priests of old, and like God's people who long ago observed the Passover, he ritually washes his hands—a baptismal image, signifying his wish to be cleansed of his sins and worthily offer the sacrifice. Remember the instructions in the First Letter to Timothy: "It is my wish, then, that in every place the men should pray, lifting up holy hands" (1 Timothy 2:8). "Holy hands" were "clean hands"; the terms were synonymous among Greek-speaking Jews. And clean hands are meant to be an outward sign of an inner purity. In baptism, we have been "washed . . . in the blood of the Lamb" (Revelation 7:14).

With our priest, we ask God to transform the gifts we place on the altar, and so transform us, and so transform the world. Saint Augustine put it very well, many, many centuries ago. At the offertory, he said, "There you are on the table, and there you are in the chalice." As the priest offers the gifts, so we offer ourselves and all that we have—our work, prayers, and Christian witness, our family life, our daily work, our leisure and our play, and even our hardships. In the words of the Second Vatican Council, "these sacrifices are most lovingly offered to the Father" with the bread and wine.

On Sundays and at special Masses, the offertory is often accompanied by a hymn. When it is, the priest quietly offers his proper part of the dialogue prayers.

The Preface and "Holy, Holy, Holy"

PRIEST: The Lord be with you.
CONGREGATION: And with your spirit.
PRIEST: Lift up your hearts.
CONGREGATION: We lift them up to the Lord.
PRIEST: Let us give thanks to the Lord our God.
CONGREGATION: It is right and just.

WHEN WE EXCHANGE THESE WORDS, as we do at every Mass, we are adding our voices to those of countless Christians since the first generations. Saint Hippolytus includes this dialogue in his account of the Roman Mass in the early 200s A.D. Saint Cyprian, just a few years later, explains these words as he described the Mass in North Africa: "The priest, by means of the preface before his prayer, prepares the minds of the people by saying, 'Lift up your hearts.' He does this so that when the people respond, 'We lift them up unto the Lord,' he may be reminded that he himself ought to think of nothing but the Lord."

So much did the early Christians love these prayers that they appear repeatedly in the homilies that have come down to us. Saint Augustine had a special regard for them and quoted them often to his congregation, urging them to lift their hearts up to the Lord, where he is enthroned in glory: "Follow then towards heaven, if you do not answer falsely when it is said, 'Lift up your hearts,' lift up your thoughts, your love, your hope: that they may not rot upon the earth. . . . For 'wherever your treasure is, there will be your heart also' [Matthew 6:21]."

We call this part of the Mass the *preface* because it is the very threshold of the most important prayer—the Eucharistic Prayer—and so it takes us to the very gate of heaven. Through the Eucharistic Prayer, Jesus becomes really present among us, as he promised; and where Jesus abides, there is heaven.

Since the root meaning of the word *Eucharist* is "thanksgiving," it is fitting that we begin our great Eucharistic Prayer on a note of gratitude. Thankfulness is indeed the dominant theme in the prayers used for the preface: "Father, all-powerful and ever-living God, we do well always and everywhere to give you thanks, through Jesus Christ our Lord."

What follows then will vary from Mass to Mass. There are prefaces for the various liturgical seasons and special prefaces for the great feasts of the year. There are prefaces for Masses commemorating the Blessed Virgin Mary, and for different categories of saints (apostles, martyrs, and so on). We give thanks for the great events of salvation history. We give thanks for the lives and witness of the saints.

Usually the preface is recited, but sometimes it is chanted

or sung. It lends itself to music because it is a great hymn of praise.

The preface is an invitation. We're approaching the most important part of the Mass, so we're invited to stop, to reflect, and to lift our hearts and minds to God. With this upward movement, we find that we on earth are joining the prayer of praise that heaven offers unceasingly. The preface concludes by reminding us that we are praying now "with all the saints and angels."

And so we sing or say:

Holy, Holy, Holy Lord God of hosts.
Heaven and earth are full of your glory.
Hosanna in the highest.
Blessed is he who comes in the name of the Lord.
Hosanna in the highest.

Like the *Gloria,* which we sang earlier, the "Holy, Holy, Holy"—sometimes called by its Latin name, the *Sanctus*—is a song that God's people learned from the angels. The angels sang the *Gloria* when they appeared upon earth. But the thrice-holy hymn is the song they sing forever in heaven. We find this revealed not just once, but twice in the Scriptures.

In the Old Testament, the Prophet Isaiah reports a vision of heaven: "Seraphim were stationed above; each of them had six wings: with two they veiled their faces, with two they veiled their feet, and with two they hovered aloft. 'Holy, holy, holy is the Lord of hosts!' they cried one to the other. 'All the earth is filled with his glory!' " (Isaiah 6:2–3).

In the New Testament, Saint John repeats this detail as he describes his own mystical experience of heaven: "The four living creatures, each of them with six wings . . . day and night they do not stop exclaiming: 'Holy, holy, holy is the Lord God almighty, who was, and who is, and who is to come' " (Revelation 4:8).

In the Mass, heaven and earth join in a single act of worship; and so the Church has long employed this song in the Mass. Pope Saint Clement of Rome mentions it in a letter written in the first century. Saint Cyril of Jerusalem said, in the fourth century: "We recite this confession of God, delivered down to us by the seraphim, so that we may share with the hosts of the world above in their hymn of praise." Cyril's contemporary and friend, Saint Gregory of Nyssa, saw this part of the Mass as symbolizing one giant leap for humankind. With Jesus, heaven has come to earth; and with his ascension, human nature has been elevated to glory. This part of the Mass represents the intersection of heaven and earth. We are at a glorious crossroads. "Heaven itself may now be walked upon by man," Saint Gregory explains. "And the creation that was once in conflict with itself—the world below against the world above—is now knit together in friendship; and we, men and women, are made to join in the angels' song, offering the worship of their praise to God."

In the Western Church, we add another acclamation to the angels' song. With the crowds who hailed Jesus as he entered Jerusalem, we say: "Hosanna . . . blessed is he who comes in the name of the Lord; hosanna in the highest!" (Matthew 21:9). And so we accompany our Lord as he leads us into the heavenly Jerusalem. We are pleased to say these words as we recall Jesus' prediction in the earthly Jerusalem: "I tell you, you will not see me again until you say, 'Blessed is he who comes in the name of the Lord' " (Matthew 23:39).

Christians have always interpreted the thrice-holy hymn as a confession of the triune God: the Blessed Trinity. The word *holy* means set apart, transcendent, heavenly as opposed to earthly; and God alone is holy by nature. God is a communion of the three divine persons who live eternally in unchanging love: the Father, the Son, and the Holy Spirit.

As we sing this hymn, we should remember that we are as close to heaven as Isaiah and Saint John were in those visions we read about in the Bible. We have lifted up our hearts to the Lord, and he has stooped down to our lowliness, as all the angels follow. We cannot help but join in their song. Long centuries ago, Saint John Chrysostom said of the Mass in his day: "The angels are present here. . . . The whole air about us is filled with angels."

Some things, like God's love, never change.

The Eucharistic Prayer

WE COME NOW TO THE moment the Church, in its General Instruction of the Roman Missal, calls "the center and summit of the entire celebration." It is when the priest does what Jesus did: he takes bread, blesses it, breaks it, and declares it to be his body, that is, the body of Jesus. The priest does this, however, in the midst of a long prayer—the longest prayer of the Mass. He does this following a minutely prescribed ritual, hallowed by two thousand years of tradition. He follows the ritual closely, because its form is something he, like Saint Paul, has "received from the Lord" (1 Corinthians 11:23). This is no place for improvisation, but for faithfulness.

We have arrived at the *Eucharistic Prayer*—also called the "Canon of the Mass," sometimes called by the Greek word *Anaphora*. *Canon* means a "measure" or "rule." *Anaphora* refers to an offering, something borne or "carried up."

The Eucharistic Prayer is indeed an offering. It is the "holy sacrifice" of the Mass. It is true that there is only one sacrifice—the self-giving of Jesus on the cross at Calvary.

Once and for all Jesus, who was the victim for our sins, offered himself up for our redemption. "For this reason he is mediator of a new covenant: since a death has taken place for deliverance from transgressions under the first covenant, those who are called may receive the promised eternal inheritance" (Hebrews 9:15).

Jesus accomplished the only sacrifice, the one great sacrifice, when, as priest and victim, he offered himself on the altar of the cross. His sacrifice need not and cannot be repeated. But it can be re-presented so that we are able, sacramentally and spiritually, to enter it and draw spiritual nourishment from it.

This should move us to the most profound prayer of gratitude—and so it does. It moves us to this prayer of *eucharistia,* which, again, is Greek for "thanksgiving."

In the United States, the congregation recognizes the sacred character of this prayer by kneeling through its entirety. As soon as we finish singing the "Holy, Holy, Holy," the faithful fall to their knees in expectation of the coming of Jesus Christ. The timing of the kneeling varies from country to country, but throughout the Western Church kneeling is observed as the appropriate posture for at least some of the Eucharistic Prayer.

In the Roman Missal, there are four primary Eucharistic Prayers the priest may choose from.

- *Eucharistic Prayer I* (also known as the Roman Canon) is based upon the great Latin liturgy of the ancient Church. In its present form, it was published by Pope Saint Pius V in 1570, but it is substantially the same as the rites described in the writings of the great fathers of the Western Church, Saint Ambrose (fourth century), Saint Augustine (fifth century), and Saint Gregory the Great (sixth century).

· *Eucharistic Prayer II* is based on a liturgy in the Greek language recorded around A.D. 215 by Saint Hippolytus of Rome. It may have been long established by the time he wrote it down. It fell into disuse for more than a millennium, but was reinstated in the second half of the twentieth century. It is brief and to the point. Eucharistic Prayer II is intended primarily for use on weekdays.

· *Eucharistic Prayer III* follows the pattern of the Roman Canon, but in a more abbreviated form. It was composed during the later part of the twentieth century.

· *Eucharistic Prayer IV* was modeled after certain liturgies of the Eastern Church. It includes a longer, very poetic retelling of the history of salvation. It begins with an account of God's life in eternity, proceeds through creation and the original sin, and then through the history of the covenants, culminating in the redemption won through the life of Jesus Christ.

In addition to these four, the Church has other Eucharistic Prayers to be used in special circumstances—for Masses of Reconciliation and for Masses with children.

The various Eucharistic Prayers differ from one another in style and content, but they share a similar solemnity and dignity. Each has its own emphasis, but they all speak the same truth, tell the same story, and accomplish the same end.

They also share certain common elements. Like so many of the prayers of the Mass, the Eucharistic Prayers are Trinitarian. In praying them, the priest, on behalf of the entire Church, addresses God the Father through Christ in the Spirit.

The Eucharistic Prayer is such a rich complex of words, gestures, and postures, involving vessels and furnishings as well, that we ought not treat it in a single chapter. We will, instead, divide our discussion as the Church has divided its own in the Missal and the Catechism. Every Eucharistic Prayer includes:

- *Thanksgiving and acclamation*—these take place most prominently in the preface and "Holy, Holy, Holy"

- *A prayer for the sending of the Holy Spirit* (also called the *epiclesis*)

- *The institution narrative*—the story of the Last Supper

- *Remembrance* (also called *anamnesis*)

- *Offering*

· *Intercessions*

· *A final doxology*

Since we already discussed thanksgiving and acclamation in the last chapter, we'll begin by looking at the invocation of the Holy Spirit.

Prayer for the Sending of the Spirit

IN EVERY EUCHARISTIC PRAYER, THE priest asks God the Father to send the Holy Spirit, the third person of the Blessed Trinity. This prayer is called the *epiclesis* (from the Greek, "to call upon"). In Eucharistic Prayer II, the priest says: "Make holy, therefore, these gifts, we pray, by sending down your Spirit upon them like the dewfall, so that they may become for us the Body and Blood of our Lord, Jesus Christ." As he does this, he draws his hands together over the gifts to evoke the hovering of the Spirit, as at the baptism of Jesus.

This is a very important prayer. For the gifts cannot be transformed by any human means, but only by the power of God. The epiclesis makes eminently clear that the Mass is primarily a work of God, and not simply a pious action or human custom. Without the power of the Holy Spirit, the Mass would not be the Mass.

By the power of the Holy Spirit, the Word was made flesh and made his dwelling among us. More than a millennium ago, Saint John of Damascus explained the Mass by comparing it with the conception of Jesus in the womb of the Virgin Mary: "You ask how the bread becomes the Body of Christ, and the wine . . . the Blood of Christ. I shall tell you: the Holy Spirit comes upon them and accomplishes what surpasses every word and thought. . . . Let it be enough for you to understand that it is by the Holy Spirit, just as it was of the Holy Virgin and by the Holy Spirit that the Lord, through and in himself, took flesh." So apt was the comparison that the Church adopted it verbatim for the Catechism (n. 1106).

It is by the Spirit that we have new life (Romans 8:15). It is only by the Spirit that we can pray to the Father (Galatians 4:6). It is by the Spirit that we know God's love in our hearts (Romans 5:5). It is the Spirit who gives us hope (Romans 15:13). Often when the New Testament speaks of the Spirit, it speaks of divine power. There is nothing the Holy

During the epiclesis, the priest extends his hands over the gifts, asking God the Father to send the Holy Spirit. © *Paul Fetters*

Spirit cannot accomplish—including the change of bread and wine into the body and blood of Christ.

The Spirit can even make us holy (Romans 15:16)—though only God is holy by nature (Revelation 15:4).

The Spirit is also the principle of unity in the Church. So the Eucharistic Prayers also include a second epiclesis, a prayer for the Spirit to come upon the people as upon the gifts. The priest prays in Eucharistic Prayer II that, "partaking of the Body and Blood of Christ, we may be gathered into one by the Holy Spirit." Similarly, in Eucharistic Prayer IV he asks that we may be "gathered into one body by the Holy Spirit." In Eucharistic Prayer III, he prays "that we, who are nourished by the Body and Blood of your Son and filled with his Holy Spirit, may become one body, one spirit in Christ." The Spirit transforms us, each of us and all of us, into Christ. We receive his body, and we become his body, by the power of the Holy Spirit.

If you visit many churches, you will often see images of the Holy Spirit above or near the altar. In the ancient and medieval Church, it was customary in some places to reserve the Eucharist in dove-shaped tabernacles suspended above the altar by a chain.

Jesus came to us to give us the Spirit, and by the Spirit we come to share God's life. That, moreover, is the Catholic understanding of grace: it is a sharing in divine life. "As fire transforms into itself everything it touches, so the Holy Spirit transforms into the divine life whatever is subjected to his power" (CCC n. 1127).

Again, this part of the Mass is our reminder that we live amid marvels, but they are no work of our own. More than a millennium and a half ago, Saint John Chrysostom said:

"He who stands at the altar does nothing, and the gifts that repose there are not the merits of a man; but the grace of the Holy Spirit is present and, descending on all, accomplishes this mysterious sacrifice. We indeed see a man [the priest], but it is God who acts through him. Nothing human takes place at this holy altar."

The Narrative of Institution

WHILE THE NEW TESTAMENT HAS several accounts of Jesus' Passion and death, the narrative always begins with the account of the Last Supper. The Gospels of Saint Matthew, Saint Mark, and Saint Luke tell the story in very similar ways, each explicitly linking the events of our redemption to the institution of the Eucharist. In Saint John's Gospel, we find an account with different emphases, but we also find Jesus' dialogue that prepared for the institution of the Eucharist. At the synagogue in Capernaum, he called himself the "bread of life . . . that comes down from heaven" (see John 6).

Saint Paul's account is similar to those of Matthew, Mark, and Luke. Paul's was probably the earliest-written of all of them—set down perhaps twenty years after the Last Supper—and he emphasizes that he is simply passing on what is already a well-known tradition: "For I received from the Lord what I also handed on to you, that the Lord Jesus, on the night he was handed over, took bread, and, after he had given thanks, broke it and said, 'This is my body

that is for you. Do this in remembrance of me.' In the same
way also the cup, after supper, saying, 'This cup is the new
covenant in my blood. Do this, as often as you drink it, in
remembrance of me.' For as often as you eat this bread and
drink the cup, you proclaim the death of the Lord until he
comes" (1 Corinthians 11:23–26).

The night before he was to undergo his Passion, Jesus
established a new memorial—a new way to recall and to remember what he was about to endure. That memorial is the
Mass, and specifically the Eucharistic Prayer. That is why
every Eucharistic Prayer in the Roman Missal includes the
institution narrative: the story of the Last Supper, drawn
from the Gospel accounts.

The original context of the new memorial was the Passover, which is itself an ancient memorial. The *seder* of the
Jews is the ritual meal established at God's command to
help the chosen people remember the events of their deliverance from Egypt and the loving-kindness of God, their
deliverer.

In that pretechnological age, there were no cameras or
camcorders, no cell phones, no tapes or disks or iPods to
hold the audio or visual data. How did people store their important memories? How did a nation like Israel preserve its
historical identity? They did this chiefly through the calendar: the celebrations and ritual reminders that recurred each
year. On festival days, people recalled what had happened to
them in the past, pondered its significance for them in the
present, and considered its implications for the future.

In the Book of Exodus we read that God instructed
Moses to institute a memorial meal—a ritual presentation of
the Passover events. The meal was closely connected with

the circumstances of the liberation. The lamb that served as a substitute for Israel's firstborn, the dinner eaten in haste while preparing for flight, these captured in ritual what God was about to effect in history.

The Lord gave a special command to repeat these ceremonies in the future: "This day shall be a memorial feast for you, which all your generations shall celebrate with pilgrimage to the Lord, as a perpetual institution. . . . Since it was on this very day that I brought your ranks out of the land of Egypt, you must celebrate this day throughout your generations as a perpetual institution" (Exodus 12:14, 17).

This series of events was lovingly preserved, for millennia, in the annual repetition of the Passover meal. As generation after generation shared the paschal lamb and unleavened bread, fathers told their children of the wonders the Lord had worked on behalf of his chosen people. Passover was more than a community festival, more than a chance to review past history. In the Passover meal, God's people knew they were with their Lord, and they renewed their family bond, their covenant with him.

As the Catechism of the Catholic Church teaches us: "In the sense of Sacred Scripture the memorial is not merely the recollection of past events but the proclamation of the mighty works wrought by God for men. In the liturgical celebration of these events, they become in a certain way present and real. This is how Israel understands its liberation from Egypt: every time Passover is celebrated, the Exodus events are made present to the memory of believers so that they may conform their lives to them" (CCC n. 1363).

In the new Passover, the Paschal Mystery of Jesus, we find a similar interplay of ritual and history. In the Old Testament, first came the offering of the Passover lamb, then the flight from Egypt. In the New Testament, first came Jesus' self-offering at the Last Supper—when he said, "This is my body"—then the crucifixion and Resurrection.

When he told his disciples to "do this," Jesus established the Last Supper as the ceremonial setting for the remembrance of our salvation. In this way, the new covenant could be renewed with every succeeding generation. We need not remain powerless in our enslavement to sin. We need not remain powerless against the finality of death.

The original Passover meal was instituted to remind Israelites of their identity as God's people. The Eucharist, too, creates a common identity for the new people of God, but it does much more as well. The Eucharist has the power to *make present* the event it memorializes—not just as a memory, but as a reality. In the New Testament, the memorial takes on new meaning. When the Church celebrates the Mass, she commemorates Christ's Passover and it is *made present:* the sacrifice Christ offered once for all on the cross remains ever present.

The Church calls us not just to a commemoration of long-ago events, as great as that might be, but also to enter the mystery itself—today. We are not bystanders, but participants.

Remembrance

Were you there when they crucified my Lord?
Were you there when they nailed him to the tree?
Were you there when they laid him in the tomb?

THE HAUNTING WORDS OF THE great American spiritual
come to mind as we reflect on the Eucharist as a *remembrance*
(in Greek, *anamnesis*).

The hymn catches a sense of our longing to *be there*, to
be present, somehow, at the foot of the cross and to receive
the redemption won for us by the blood that flowed from
Jesus' hands and feet and side. It's as if remembering him is
not enough. We want to be with him.

We have no time machine. We cannot be physically
present at Calvary, but there is a real sense—a sacramental
and spiritual sense—in which we *are there* as we share in the
Eucharist. Read Paul's Letter to the Hebrews, and you'll see
that Jesus now presides as high priest in heaven, presenting
the gift of himself to the Father: his body, blood, soul, and
divinity. He holds nothing back from the Father.

Nor does he hold anything back from us. In heaven, God's self-gift is eternal, complete, and perfect. On earth, the very sign of that self-giving is the crucifix that stands by the altar. Jesus' self-giving on the cross was to be everlasting, complete, and perfect. The re-presentation of that gift is the Mass. There, Jesus gives us his body, blood, soul, and divinity in the Eucharist. He shares his life with us. And we join in his great offering to the Father. "Through him let us continually offer God a sacrifice of praise" (Hebrews 13:15).

Jesus knew we would want to be with him, wherever he should go. He himself wanted to be with us forever. So he made his promise: "And behold, I am with you always, until the end of the age" (Matthew 28:20), and he established the means for us to enjoy his presence. It is the Eucharist.

We are not simply bystanders at this memorial. We are partakers in the Passover of Jesus Christ. This new ritual instituted at the Last Supper gives us the body of Christ. It makes us the body of Christ. Since Christ has given himself as our spiritual food, we "come to share in the divine nature" (2 Peter 1:4).

> When the Church celebrates the Eucharist, the memorial of her Lord's death and Resurrection, this central event of salvation becomes really present and "the work of our redemption is carried out" (*Lumen Gentium,* 3). (*Ecclesia de Eucharistia,* 11)

Were you there? Yes, you *are* there. You are with him, whenever the Church remembers—whenever you go to Mass.

The First Elevation of the Host and Chalice

"And just as Moses lifted up the serpent in the desert, so must the Son of Man be lifted up, so that everyone who believes in him may have eternal life" (John 3:14–15).

"When you lift up the Son of Man, then you will realize that I AM, and that I do nothing on my own, but I say only what the Father taught me" (John 8:28).

"And when I am lifted up from the earth, I will draw everyone to myself" (John 12:32).

We are his beloved disciples, whom he has drawn to the Mount of the Ascension: "as they were looking on, he was lifted up" (Acts 1:9).

When the priest consecrates the bread, it is no longer bread, though it keeps the appearance of bread. It is the body of Christ. "The bread that we break, is it not a participation in the body of Christ?" (1 Corinthians 10:16). It is indeed the body of Christ, and the priest raises it up as a perfect offering to the Father.

When the priest consecrates the chalice of wine, it no longer holds wine, though the contents of the chalice keep the appearance of wine. The chalice now contains the blood of Christ. "The cup of blessing that we bless, is it not a participation in the blood of Christ?" (1 Corinthians 10:16). It is indeed a communion in Christ's blood. The priest elevates the chalice as a perfect offering to the Father.

This part of the Mass is known as the "major elevation." At each elevation, first the host and then the chalice, you will see some people bow, others gaze at the elements, and still others whisper prayers under their breath (a favorite is

After consecrating the bread so it becomes the body of Christ, the priest elevates the host. © *Paul Fetters*

THE HOST AND CHALICE

that of the Apostle Thomas: "My Lord and my God" [John 20:28]).

To know Jesus is to love him. To gaze upon him is to be overwhelmed by that love. Knowing what we know—about his memorial, about his real presence—how can we help but adore him?

The bells that are rung at many churches during each elevation strike the ears as a fanfare for this heavenly King, who comes to us so humbly.

The Mystery of Faith

THE PRIEST CALLS US TO proclaim "the mystery of faith." The congregation responds with one of several short statements:

We proclaim your death, O Lord, and profess your Resurrection until you come again.

When we eat this bread and drink this cup, we proclaim your death, O Lord, until you come again.

Save us, Savior of the world, for by your cross and Resurrection you have set us free.

The response is a summary of the Paschal Mystery—Jesus' Passion, death, Resurrection, and glorification—in its past, present, and future dimensions. We affirm the historical truth: cross, death, and rising. We affirm the present reality: the bread of life and the cup of salvation. We ac-

knowledge its saving power. And we look to its future fulfillment, begun now in the Eucharist, when Christ comes
in glory.

The Church identifies this mystery as the center of the
whole Christian experience. Pope Benedict XVI noted that
Christ redeemed mankind "principally by the Paschal Mystery of his blessed passion, resurrection from the dead and
glorious ascension, whereby 'dying, he destroyed our death
and, rising, he restored our life.'" The Church celebrates
the Paschal Mystery by "reading also 'in all the Scriptures
those things which referred to himself' (Luke 24:27), celebrating the Eucharist in which 'the victory and triumph of
his death are again made present,' and at the same time giving thanks 'to God for his indescribable gift' (2 Corinthians
9:15) in Christ Jesus, 'to the praise of his glory' (Ephesians
1:12), through the power of the Holy Spirit."

In the liturgy the victory and triumph of Christ's death
are made present, so that we can say, as does the Second
Vatican Council, "The Liturgy is the summit toward which
the activity of the Church is directed; at the same time it is
the font from which all her power flows."

All the mysteries of faith are revealed to us within a single mystery: the Paschal Mystery. We enter that mystery
through the Eucharist. Christ our Passover Lamb is sacrificed *today*, because his sacrifice was once for all. *That's* the
mystery made present—re-presented now.

In the Jubilee Year at the turn of the millennium, Pope
John Paul II marveled at this gift as he offered Mass with
his brother bishops in Jerusalem, in the Upper Room where
Jesus celebrated the Last Supper.

At every Holy Mass, we proclaim this "mystery of faith," which for two millennia has nourished and sustained the Church as she makes her pilgrim way amid the persecutions of the world and the consolations of God, proclaiming the cross and death of the Lord until he comes. . . .

This is the "mystery of faith" which we proclaim in every celebration of the Eucharist. Jesus Christ, the priest of the new and eternal covenant, has redeemed the world by his Blood. Risen from the dead, he has gone to prepare a place for us in his Father's house. In the Spirit who has made us God's beloved children, in the unity of the Body of Christ, we await his return with joyful hope.

The season and the surroundings made that Mass special for the pope. He reminded everyone, however, that the saving truth applies to every Mass, no matter where it is celebrated, no matter when.

Eucharistic Prayers

"BLESS THESE GIFTS . . . WHICH WE offer you first of all for your holy catholic Church." So says the priest when he recites the first Eucharistic Prayer. "And [bless] all those who, holding to the truth, hand on the catholic and apostolic faith."

"Catholic" is what we have called our Church since the first generation of Christianity. Saint Ignatius of Antioch used the phrase in A.D. 107, and so did many more authors in his century and the next. The word *catholic* means "universal," a term that well describes the scope of our concerns during the Mass, and especially during the Eucharistic Prayer.

The Church is *catholic* because Christ is present in her, wherever she may be. As Saint Ignatius wrote, "Where there is Christ Jesus, there is the Catholic Church." The Catholic Church is also a church for all peoples in all places and at all times. It continues to teach all that Christ taught.

"Catholic" denotes not a sect or a denomination, but a church as big as the world and as vast as time. That's why we offer such a range of petitions along with the Lord's body and blood during the Eucharistic Prayer.

The Eucharist is the prayer of the whole Church. We thank God the Father for his mercy in redeeming the world. We thank him especially for sending the Son into the world to be one of us. That is why, in the course of this long prayer, we sketch out the history of God's saving acts.

We also raise our prayer in intercession for the whole world. There is a universal, catholic quality to the petitions of the Eucharistic Prayer. We seek the fulfillment of the longings, expectations, and needs of the whole Church and the whole universe. Saint Paul described the matter well: "We know that *all creation* is groaning in labor pains even until now" (Romans 8:22). We feel helpless in the face of so much need, but the Holy Spirit "comes to the aid of our weakness; for we do not know how to pray as we ought, but the Spirit itself intercedes with inexpressible groanings" (Romans 8:26).

So we pray for the Church "spread throughout the world." We pray for mercy, salvation. We pray for the living and the dead. We pray for "the whole order of bishops, all the clergy, those who make this offering, those gathered here before you, your entire people, and all who seek you with a sincere heart." We pray that "the whole of creation" may be "freed from the corruption of sin and death" and so may glorify God.

The Mass is the universal prayer. Saint Justin Martyr wrote that, by his time, A.D. 150, the Mass was offered by Christians of every race and nation in the known world. Christianity was hardly more than a century old, and the

Mass was already catholic. It was already offered wherever people could go to tell the good news.

It still is. We are Catholic because our love is universal. Our care is universal as well. Catholics are never narrow in their prayer. Though we arrive at Mass with all our private hopes and worries, we join them with the intentions of the whole world, and with Christ, and in Christ, we make our intercession with the Father.

The Great Amen

WE MENTIONED, SEVERAL CHAPTERS AGO, that only two Hebrew words have survived, untranslated, in common use in the Mass. One is *Alleluia;* the other is *Amen.* By this point in the Mass, we have already encountered the word *Amen* many times. It is the last word in most prayers—a kind of prayerful punctuation.

The word *Amen* completes a prayer. It signifies our consent to all the words that preceded it.

Jesus used it also as a preface to especially solemn teachings. He did this especially in connection with the doctrine of the Eucharist. Four times in his Bread of Life discourse you'll find him pronouncing a double *Amen.* Consider two examples:

> "Amen, amen, I say to you, it was not Moses who gave the bread from heaven; my Father gives you the true bread from heaven" (John 6:32).

> "Amen, amen, I say to you, unless you eat the flesh of

the Son of Man and drink his blood, you do not have life within you" (John 6:53).

Amen, in this sacred context, means "truly." It means "I believe." It means "Yes." In Jesus' culture, it was pronounced as the affirmation of an oath. Those who pronounced it put their lives on the line. They committed themselves to a serious undertaking. They pledged their full and unreserved faith.

Curiously, it also means "Jesus." In the Book of Revelation, we find an angel refer to Jesus as "The *Amen,* the faithful and true witness" (Revelation 3:14).

There are many *Amens* in the course of the Mass, but this is the great one because it follows the final doxology of the Eucharistic Prayer. We spoke a bit about doxologies in

At the end of the Eucharistic Prayer, the chalice and paten, with the body and blood of Christ, are elevated as the congregation sings the *Great Amen.* © *Paul Fetters*

our discussion of the *Gloria*. The doxology usually serves as a finale to a prayer. In the case of the Church's great prayer, the Eucharistic Prayer, the doxology is a grand finale indeed. The priest intones:

> Through him, and with him, and in him, to you, O
> God, almighty Father, in the unity of the Holy Spirit,
> is all honor and glory, for ever and ever.

And those words call forth from all believers a *Great Amen*.

What is so great about our *Amen*? We find a clue in the ancient oracle of the Old Testament prophet Malachi (1:11), who foresaw the day of our sacrifice and rejoiced.

> *For from the rising of the sun, even to its setting,*
> my name is great among the nations;
> *And everywhere they bring sacrifice to my name,*
>   *and a pure offering;*
> *For great is my name among the nations,*
>   *says the Lord of hosts.*

The Lord's Prayer

AT THE BEGINNING OF JESUS' ministry, his disciples asked him, "Lord, teach us to pray," and Jesus delighted in this request. He responded by giving them the prayer we call the "Our Father" or "Lord's Prayer" (see Luke 11:1–4). The Church celebrates this as the most cherished prayer and gives it a prominent place at Mass. Indeed, it has been part of the worship of Christian assemblies since the very beginning of Christianity. The most ancient guide to the liturgy, the *Didache* from the first century, gives instructions for praying the Lord's Prayer daily. And the early Christians consistently connected this prayer with the Mass. Tertullian in the second century, Saint Cyprian in the third century, and many others taught that the petition for "our daily bread" was a plea before God for the gift of the Eucharist.

The prayer has rightly been called a "summary of the whole Gospel." There are few prayers that should be so regularly on our lips and in our heart. There is no prayer so appropriate for this particular part of the Mass. We could write a book on the Lord's Prayer alone, and many authors already have! Here we would like to emphasize how the "Our Father" prepares us for Communion.

As the priest calls us to recite this prayer, he recognizes the audacity of what we are about to do. "At the Savior's command and formed by divine teaching, we dare to say . . ." What is it that we *dare* to say? "Our Father."

Those opening words bring us face to face with the extraordinary revelation of Jesus Christ. He alone is the true, natural Son of God. Remember, in the creed, we proclaimed him as "God from God, light from light, true God from true God"—the only begotten Son of the Father.

Yet he came among us so that he could make us co-heirs to his inheritance (see Romans 8:17, Galatians 3:29, Ephesians 3:6, Titus 3:7, and many other Scriptures). We share in his death and Resurrection through our baptism and our participation in the Eucharist. We become adopted children of God because we share the life of the natural Son of God. We share his life because he came to share ours. Saint Paul made this very clear: "But when the fullness of time had come, God sent his Son, born of a woman, born under the law, to ransom those under the law, so that we might receive adoption. As proof that you are children, God sent the spirit of his Son into our hearts, crying out, 'Abba, Father!' So you are no longer a slave but a child, and if a child then also an heir, through God" (Galatians 4:4–7).

We have been called to this unique relationship with God out of our former sinful state. Each person, with the exception of Mary who was preserved from all stain of sin by a singular grace of God in view of the merits of her Son, is born in original sin, and into a world damaged by sin. But God "delivered us from the power of darkness and transferred us to the kingdom of his beloved Son, in whom we have redemption, the forgiveness of sins" (Colossians 1:13–14). Saint Paul speaks of this justifying mercy of God often, especially in his Letter to the Romans.

The opening of the Lord's Prayer reminds us that we can call God "our Father" because of the generous outpouring of the Holy Spirit on everyone who proclaims Jesus as Lord. The first of all God's gifts is the gift of himself. He desires to give himself to us perfectly in eternal life. But that giving begins now and arrives in a supreme way in the Mass.

There is a world of difference between knowing God as "our Father" and knowing him as "Creator" or "Lord." "Father" denotes a loving, familiar, familial relationship. It means he is our protector, friend, guide, teacher, provider, doing everything he does for us with a tender and personal affection. He is with us, transforming and making us children by adoption and sharers in his nature. He is present to unite us to himself (see John 17:22–23). He is present that he may be known. He wishes us all to grow in holiness and the life of prayer, so that we may more and more taste his presence as saints and mystics of every age have done.

Though he remains God and we remain creatures, somehow we are closely joined to him. We share his life. We remain always finite and distinct from him who is the infinite Lord of all. But the mystery that transcends our understanding is that somehow God becomes so close to us that we can call him Father.

If God is our Father, then we must be brothers and sisters. This truth is at the heart of the Christian community—the Church. We are one with each other because we are one with Jesus the Lord. While there are many ways we might identify with other groups—our blood ties, ethnic origins, cultural interests—there is one reality that supersedes all these other bonds: union with each other in Christ.

To pray to God as "our Father" is to recognize that we have responsibilities to each other as members of the same family. We are not merely components of a cultural, political, economic, or social entity. We are a faith community. If our faith is strong enough, we'll recognize how deep our spiritual bonds are; and then we can accomplish that communion, that family life, that manifestation of the kingdom of God that Jesus calls for when he urges us to name God as "our Father."

We call God our Father, but still we recognize his utter transcendence. We pray, "Our Father, who art in heaven," and we "hallow" his name. We proclaim his name to be "Holy," that is, "set apart." As close as we can now draw to the divine life—through the Holy Spirit and in Jesus Christ—God is still utterly beyond us, transcendent, all-holy and infinite, with limitless power and majesty. In the creed we have professed our belief in the "Father almighty." In the *Gloria* we have sung about the grandeur of that truth. At the beginning of the Eucharistic Prayer, we hallowed God's name three times over: Holy, holy, holy! The Church unceasingly proclaims the glory of God.

No creature is worthy by nature to draw near to such glory, never mind speak in its presence. But the same divine perfection is also the root of perfect mercy, which heals sinners and calls them to communion to be divinized (see 2 Peter 1:4).

When we pray to "our Father" we recognize that it is God's holiness that attracts the human heart. It attracts us because of the goodness it implies, a goodness of such intensity that it dispels any servile fear and touches the sinful heart with awe and reverence.

The splendor and holiness of God must be taken seriously. God is holy and requires holiness and will judge us on how well we correspond to the holiness he has shared with us. Thus, the fear of the Lord is the beginning of wisdom (see Proverbs 1:7). Still, that "fear" is not the cowering of a slave, but rather the awe of a child before a parent who can do so much, be so much, and give so much.

The disciples asked a simple question. They wanted guidance in prayer, maybe a tip on technique. Imagine their excitement when Jesus gave them not words of encouragement or mere methods, but the actual words of the prayer itself—perfect words that themselves reveal a new relationship—words that beg a familial communion that comes, very soon, through the grace of "our daily bread," the Holy Eucharist.

So we pray this prayer with special attention when we pray it in the Mass. As we do, we pray in continuity with the apostles and through them with Jesus as he gathers his Church. We pray in a way that is guaranteed to turn our hearts and minds to God.

The Sign of Peace

"GREET ONE ANOTHER WITH A holy kiss," said Saint Paul (Romans 16:16). In fact, he said it repeatedly. The phrase appears at the end of both his letters to the Corinthians as well as his Letter to the Thessalonians. It must have been a commonplace statement of the apostles, because Saint Peter also says, "Greet one another with a loving kiss. Peace to all of you who are in Christ" (1 Peter 5:14).

So, even today, when we meet for Mass, our priests invite us to "offer each other the sign of peace." The sign will vary from culture to culture. For some people it is a hand-shake, for others a brief embrace, for still others a courteous bow. We should do what is culturally appropriate. As Saint Ambrose said in the fourth century: "When I am at Milan, I do as they do at Milan; but when I go to Rome, I do as Rome does."

In Ambrose's day, the Sign of Peace was already a well-established part of the Mass. Saint Justin Martyr speaks of it in his description of the Mass in the second century, and Tertullian speaks of it just a little later. Saint Cyril of

Jerusalem, a contemporary of Saint Ambrose, said that in his Church the deacon called out for the people to "embrace one another, and let us greet one another." He went on to explain: "This kiss is the sign that our souls are united and that we banish all remembrance of injury."

Saint Cyril, like many of the early Christians, makes the connection between this simple gesture and the words of the Lord Jesus: "Therefore, if you bring your gift to the altar, and there recall that your brother has anything against you, leave your gift there at the altar, go first and be reconciled with your brother, and then come and offer your gift" (Matthew 5:23–24).

This is a crucial moment in the Mass. We have just dared to call God "Our Father." We soon will dare to approach his altar and receive his body and blood as our own. He demands that, before we take another step toward communion with "our Father," we must make peace with our siblings in God's family.

The gesture we make—whatever it may be—must be a sign of a deeper and more pervasive peace in our lives. We are not just declaring our peace with the person who happens to be in the seat next to us. We make a sign that we are at peace with everyone—even those people whom we may count as rivals, opponents, or adversaries. In the course of life, people will disagree with one another; but that does not mean they must cease respecting one another or loving one another. We place a premium on charity; and with charity comes peace. Jesus made such peace a precondition of a truly Holy Communion.

Peace also presupposes justice. We cannot honestly say we are at peace with our neighbors if we are not doing what we can to make sure they are getting adequate food, clothing, and shelter. This is only just. God created the goods of the world intending them to be distributed among his creatures. If we are overfed and clothed in finery while others are hungry and cold, then we cannot say we are living justly. Saint John Chrysostom spoke of these matters often when he spoke of the Mass: "Do you wish to honor the body of Christ? Do not ignore him when he is naked. Do not pay him homage in the temple clad in silk only then to neglect him outside where he suffers cold and nakedness. He who said: 'This is my body' is the same one who said: 'You saw me hungry and you gave me no food' and 'Whatever you did to the least of my brothers you did also to me.' . . . What good is it if the Eucharistic table is overloaded with golden chalices, when he is dying of hunger? Start by satisfying his hunger, and then with what is left you may adorn the altar as well."

The Sign of Peace has occupied different moments in the liturgy, down the centuries. Some churches placed it nearer the offertory. The Roman Church tended to give it the place we give it today, to make the clear connection between earthly peace and Holy Communion. A fifth-century pope, Saint Innocent I, said that it is a sign that we agree with everything that has already been accomplished in the course of the Mass.

Some people are reticent about making the Sign of Peace. For those whose immune systems are compromised by illness, medical treatment, or age, a simple handshake could mean greater vulnerability to infection. We should respect their wishes if they prefer simply to nod in our direction. We should greet their gesture with our warmest smile. That can be, all the more, a Sign of Peace.

The Lamb of God

As the Mass approaches its dramatic climax—Holy Communion—the ritual connections to the ancient Passover grow ever stronger. Now, when the faithful are about to step forward for the sacrament, we proclaim Jesus repeatedly as the "Lamb of God." In doing so, we echo the cry of Saint John the Baptist when he saw Jesus approaching. Twice he cried out, "Behold, the Lamb of God!" (see John 1:29 and 1:36).

In speaking of the old Passover, Saint Luke reminds us of its association with the sacrificial lamb and with unleavened bread. He tells us of "the day of the Feast of Unleavened Bread arrived, the day for sacrificing the Passover lamb" (Luke 22:7). Saint Paul carries that connection over to the new Passover, the Paschal Mystery of Jesus Christ: "our paschal lamb, Christ, has been sacrificed. Therefore let us celebrate the feast . . . with the unleavened bread of sincerity and truth" (1 Corinthians 5:7–8).

In the mystical visions of the Book of Revelation, we find the courts of heaven worshipping at an altar, and the object of their worship is the divine Lamb, Jesus Christ. Read chapter five of that book. The Lamb seems to have been slain, yet he is alive, and triumphant, and he rules both heaven and earth. Heaven and earth together worship him with hymns, prayers, blessings, readings, incense, and a *Great Amen*. Then turn to chapter nineteen, and you'll see that the worship has become a "wedding feast of the Lamb" (Revelation 19:9).

The original Passover marked a new life for the chosen people, as they "passed over" from slavery to freedom, from Egypt to the promised land. Our new Passover, Jesus Christ, marks an even greater change to an even greater new life. Through this feast the Lamb accomplishes a marriage of heaven and earth, of God and the Church. This is the meaning of our Holy Communion.

While the congregation prays or sings the "Lamb of God," the priest breaks the host and mingles a small portion with the Precious Blood of Christ in the chalice. © *Paul Fetters*

We have returned to the Passover theme many times throughout the Mass. In the *Gloria* we addressed Jesus as "Lamb of God." Here, however, he is called the Lamb four times in a very short period of time, three times in this prayer and once in the priest's acclamation afterward. The words of the Mass are drawing us deeply into the drama of our salvation. The prayers compress all of salvation history to a single point in our lives.

This is our Passover. It is your Passover. It is intensely personal. Nevertheless, it is intensely communal. We draw closer together as we draw closer to Jesus.

While we are praying or singing the "Lamb of God," the priest breaks the host and mingles a small portion of it with the Precious Blood of Christ, which fills the chalice. The sacrificial action is complete, and all that is left is for the Victim, our "sacrificial Lamb," to be consumed.

Like the words of Saint Luke and Saint Paul, the prayers of the Church identify the Lamb with the bread. In fact, in the Eastern Churches the Eucharistic bread is not called the "host," but rather by the Greek and Slavonic words for "lamb." The "Lamb of God" prayer entered the Mass in the West through the efforts of a man from the East, Pope Saint Sergius I, a Syrian who reigned in the seventh century.

"I Am Not Worthy"

WE CONTINUE THE PASSOVER THEME as the priest holds up the host and chalice and calls the congregation to "Behold the Lamb of God." He adds, "Behold him who takes away the sins of the world. Blessed are those called to the supper of the Lamb."

Then, together with the people, he says: "Lord, I am not worthy that you should enter under my roof, but only say the word and my soul shall be healed."

That is a powerful prayer. It is an honest prayer. If we have been following the Mass closely, by now we should have a clear view of *who God is* and *who we are* in relation to him. God is the Creator, and we are his creatures. He has no obligation to share his nature with us. He is eternal and infinite, and we are temporal and finite. What could he have to do with us? He is holy, and we are sinners. By our disobedience, we have forfeited the privilege of living in his presence.

We are not worthy. This statement is simply our logical inference based on what we've seen so far.

The prayer is taken almost verbatim from the Gospel of Saint Matthew. It appears in a chapter that shows Jesus' immense power as a healer. First he cured a leper just by declaring him "clean" (Matthew 8:2–3).

Then a Roman official approached him—a Roman, a Gentile, and so a man who had no claim to God's promises to his chosen people. The man seeks help not for himself, but for a beloved employee: "Lord, my servant is lying at home paralyzed, suffering dreadfully" (Matthew 8:6). Jesus consents to curing the young man. But the servant protests: "Lord, I am not worthy to have you enter under my roof; only say the word and my servant will be healed" (Matthew 8:8).

Those words "amazed" Jesus, who extolled the faith of this Gentile.

Like that long-ago centurion, we see Jesus and are moved to ask for mercy, for healing. We demonstrate our faith by our approach. Like the centurion, we plead our unworthiness. We can rest confident of Jesus' response. It will be as we read in the Gospel. He has the power to cure our spiritual and moral ills, and he has the will to do so. If we ask him to heal us, he says the word and our souls "shall be healed."

Holy Communion

ALL OF OUR PRAYERS THUS far have served to bring us to the moment of Holy Communion, the moment when God incarnate joins himself with us, mingling his body and blood with ours, sharing his soul and divinity with our poor humanity.

Much of the language of the Mass has been exalted, the movements sometimes elaborate.

Yet now, as the drama reaches its climax, the rite becomes spare and simple. It is beautiful in its simplicity. It is profound in its simplicity. But it is nonetheless simple.

Each communicant bows reverently while approaching the priest.

The priest holds up a host and says, "The body of Christ."

The communicant says, "Amen," and receives Jesus.

The Church has preserved the rite in this simplicity since the earliest centuries. In the fourth century, Saint Ambrose described it in terms that still apply today: "The priest says to you, 'The body of Christ.' And you say, 'Amen.'" From the same generation, we find descriptions of the rite in Jerusalem and North Africa, and they are exactly the same.

In the West we do have options for our manner of receiving the host. We may receive on the tongue, or we may receive in the hand. If we receive on the tongue, we should open our mouth wide and move our tongue forward, making it visible and accessible to the priest, deacon, or the extraordinary minister of Holy Communion who is assisting him.

If we receive in the hand, we may follow the instructions given by Saint Cyril of Jerusalem in the fourth century. He said to make one hand "a throne" for the other. "Then hollow your palm, and receive the body of Christ, saying over it, 'Amen.'" A right-handed person would place the right hand under the left, then receive the host in the palm of the left hand. After stepping to the side, the communicant

Catholics may receive the Eucharist directly on the tongue
or in the hand. © *Paul Fetters*

should pick up the host with the right hand and consume it. (A left-handed person would place the left hand under the right, then receive the host in the palm of the right hand. Stepping to the side, the communicant would pick up the host with the left hand and consume it.)

Saint Cyril exhorts his flock to be "careful not to lose any small particle; for whatever you lose is as much a loss to you as if it were one of your own limbs. Tell me, if anyone gave you grains of gold, would you not hold them with utmost care, on guard against losing any? Will you not take greater care not to lose a crumb of what is more precious than gold or jewels?"

Saint Cyril continued: "Then, after partaking the body of Christ, draw near to the cup of his blood . . . bowing reverently and saying, 'Amen.' Then bring a blessing upon

Catholics may receive the Eucharist in the hand or directly
on the tongue. © *Paul Fetters*

yourself by partaking of the blood of Christ." We sip from
the chalice and return it to the minister who handed it to us.

It is an easy thing to follow such a simple rite. This simplicity leaves our mind free for prayer. So we should approach Holy Communion in a recollected way and try not
to be distracted, even if we catch sight of people we know.
We should keep our focus on Jesus and prepare ourselves for
an intimate encounter.

After Communion, as we wait for the remaining worshippers to receive, we should intensify our prayer, knowing that, at that moment, we are as close to Jesus as it is
possible to be.

The decision to distribute Communion under one kind
or both belongs to the priest who celebrates Mass (and to
his bishop). The sacramental sign is richer and more complete when the congregation receives the host and from the
chalice. In that form, the Mass has more the appearance of
a meal, a banquet—especially that sacred meal when Jesus
said, "Take . . . eat" and "Take . . . drink."

Sometimes, however—in flu season, for example—the
local Church or any individual priest may decide that it is
best not to share a common chalice. His decision should be
respected.

Christ, after all, is fully present under each species alone.
When we receive the host by itself, we receive Jesus' body
and blood, soul and divinity. When we receive from the
chalice alone, we receive Jesus' body and blood, soul and divinity. People with severe sensitivities to wheat, for example, can receive only from the chalice; but, doing so, they
receive *all* of Jesus and *all* the grace of the sacrament.

Should I Receive?

SOMETIMES AT MASS, WE MAY notice people holding back from receiving Holy Communion. They remain in their pews when others go forward, or they indicate to the priest or deacon that they will not receive. This is especially common at wedding and funeral Masses, when a strong sense of duty or obligation draws non-Catholics and non-practicing Catholics to church.

You and I may not know the reasons they decline the sacrament, but we should respect their thoughtfulness and integrity. In their way, they are recognizing the importance of the Mass.

To respond to the Lord's invitation to eat his flesh and drink his blood, the believer must be prepared. Saint Paul urges us to examine our conscience: "Therefore whoever eats the bread or drinks the cup of the Lord unworthily will have to answer for the body and blood of the Lord" (1 Corinthians 11:27). Before we approach the table of the Lord it is important to reflect on our life, ask God's forgiveness for our failings and—if necessary due to serious sin—to avail ourselves of sacramental confession.

The *United States Catholic Catechism for Adults* tells us "all must examine their consciences as to their worthiness to receive the Body and Blood of our Lord. This examination includes fidelity to the moral teaching of the Church in personal and public life."

Recent polls indicate that a significant number of Catholics do not have a complete understanding of the Eucharist and specifically the real presence of Christ in the Blessed Sacrament. Whatever the cause of such misunderstanding of the faith, each person who approaches the table of the Lord needs to recognize the significance of this action and the importance of spiritual preparation. It sometimes becomes the task of older members of the family to review with youngsters what is happening at Mass and who we receive in Holy Communion. Grandparents have in some instances a unique and privileged role as teachers of the faith in an age when the awareness of the real presence seems to be diminished.

Again, at weddings, funerals, and other special occasions, we may find ourselves at church with people who do not share our faith—or people who are estranged from the Church. At such times, we may face a temptation to avoid awkwardness by inviting them to receive the Eucharist. Those who are not in full communion with the Church, however, are not permitted to participate at the table of the Lord as if they were full members, sharers in the full sacramental life of the Church. The reason is simple. Reception of Holy Communion proclaims publicly that the one receiving the Lord is a member of the Catholic Church. To do so while not being Catholic is to be a witness to something that is not true.

To help both Catholics and those who do not share our faith respond appropriately, the United States Conference of Catholic Bishops issued some years ago guidelines for Receiving Holy Communion (see page 51). These remind Catholics of their need to be properly disposed, to have fasted for an hour, and to seek to live in charity and love with our neighbors. For other Christians, the text says: "We pray that our common baptism and the action of the Holy Spirit in this Eucharist will draw us closer to one another and begin to dispel the sad divisions which separate us. We pray that these will lessen and finally disappear, in keeping with Christ's prayer for us 'that they may all be one' (John 17:21).

Because Catholics believe that the celebration of the Eucharist is a sign of the reality of the oneness of faith, life, and worship, members of those churches with whom we are not yet fully united are ordinarily not admitted to Holy Communion."

We should thank God that such an overwhelmingly generous gift was given to us—but we must also challenge ourselves to live so as to receive our Lord reverently and frequently.

In a tradition that is enjoying a resurgence in some parishes, a number of people are once again coming to church early to prepare themselves quietly for the spiritual experience of the Mass. This is one small practice that each of us can adopt as a way of strengthening our own faith and appreciating more deeply the mystery we are invited to enter as we approach the presence of God with us in the Eucharist. Those few minutes of quiet preparation have the spiritual effect of opening our hearts to the Lord. Each Sunday we can quietly, in our hearts, prepare a way for the Lord. All it takes is a little time to recollect our thoughts, recall what we are doing, and thank God for the real presence of Jesus Christ in the Eucharist.

The Cleansing of the Vessels

AFTER COMMUNION, THERE IS A bustle of quiet and orderly activity in the sanctuary. If any of the Precious Blood remains in the chalice, the priest and deacons consume it,

After Communion, the priest or deacon cleans the ciboria, chalices, and other vessels. The chalice is purified with water, which the priest or deacon then drinks. © *Paul Fetters*

assisted by the extraordinary ministers if necessary (where this is permitted by the local bishop).

The priest or deacon will then take water and cleanse the inside of the vessels: the ciboria, patens, chalices, and so on. If a fragment of the host sticks to the priest's fingers, he wipes or washes his fingers over the paten. Meanwhile, he also looks for fragments that may have fallen onto the altar cloths.

The priest or deacon purifies the chalice with water and then drinks the water. The paten is usually wiped clean with the purificator.

These simple, homey actions are a profound witness to Jesus' real presence in the sacrament. If we believe that he is entirely present in every drop and every crumb, then the priest must take special care to consume every drop and crumb.

The Prayer After Communion

AFTER THE PURIFICATION OF THE vessels, the priest recites a very brief prayer, plain in its practicality. The theme of the prayer usually refers to the Holy Communion just consumed and to its effects and benefits in us.

The Blessing and Dismissal

DOES IT SEEM STRANGE TO you that "the Mass" takes its name from its final words, the dismissal? The Latin words are *Ite, missa est.* In modern English they're rendered, "Go forth, the Mass is ended."

Does it seem strange that the Mass ends so abruptly after Communion? We reach the highest peak possible, then suddenly we're sent away after the barest blessing: "May almighty God bless you: the Father, and the Son, and the Holy Spirit."

Then it's over.

Who could blame us if we felt like Saint Peter? He saw Jesus transfigured on the mountaintop and wished to remain there forever, setting up booths on the site (see Mark 9:5).

If you have wondered about these matters, you are not the first. Before he was elevated to the papacy, Pope Benedict XVI was a famous theologian, who pondered the great mysteries of Christianity. His name was Joseph Ratzinger. He, too, turned his attention to the suddenness of our dismissal from worship; and he found the key to understand-

The Mass ends as it began: with a Sign of the Cross. © *Paul Fetters*

ing that moment in a Gospel story. It was the story of Jesus' encounter, on the day of his Resurrection, with two disciples who were walking from Jerusalem to the town of Emmaus. Jesus approached the two disciples, who were at first prevented from recognizing him.

The disciples were downcast before they met the mysterious stranger. He walked with them awhile and entered their conversation, probing them with questions, drawing out their response. He listened to them as they poured out their hearts. "Then beginning with Moses and all the prophets, he interpreted to them what referred to him in all the Scriptures" (Luke 24:27).

When the disciples arrived at their destination, they invited the man to stay with them. It was only when he "took bread, said the blessing, broke it, and gave it to them" (24:30) that they recognized him as Jesus. "He was made known to them in the breaking of the bread" (24:35). Then he vanished from their sight, and they were left to tell the good news to their fellow disciples. They "set out at once" for Jerusalem (24:33).

This event, on that first Christian Passover, showed us the completion of the Paschal Mystery. Joseph Ratzinger examined the scene: "First we have the searching of the Scriptures, explained and made present by the risen Lord; their minds enlightened, the disciples are moved to invite the Lord to stay with them, and he responds by breaking the bread for his disciples, giving them his presence and then withdrawing again, sending them out as his messengers."

Isn't this our experience? We come to Mass, perhaps distracted by a thousand and one troubles and concerns of everyday life. Then Jesus draws close to us, though not in an overwhelming way. By the prayers of the Mass, he draws out our response. He gives us words to express our sorrow, our pleas, our praise. Then he opens the Scriptures to us. He gives us himself in the most intimate way. And then comes our dis-missal, our com-mission. These words come from the same Latin root as our beloved *Mass*.

What we receive in the Mass we must now take into the world. The challenging thing about Christian faith is that we cannot hold on to it unless we give it away—unless we share it with others. We have received Christ, and he has mingled his flesh with ours. His blood courses through us and gives life to our bodies—gives his life to our bodies! We become his face and voice and hands and feet as we walk out into the crowded sidewalks, as we return to our homes and neighborhoods, and we report for another workday.

We can mark the moments till our next opportunity to go to Mass. But in the meantime we must live the Mass. This is what the Church means when it describes the Mass as the "source and summit" of Christian life. The Eucharist gives us the grace we need to live in the world, but live for heaven. Our life in the world should be our preparation for the next Eucharist. We try to live in a way that is worthy of Jesus' constant presence. We try to live in a way that manifests our communion with Jesus.

Saint Francis de Sales tried to live his life so that whenever anyone asked him what he was doing, he could honestly say, "I'm preparing for Mass." A twentieth-century theologian, F. X. Durrwell, took that thought a step further. He said he wanted to be so united with Jesus' self-giving that he could always honestly say: "I'm offering Mass."

We offer ourselves when we go to Mass. We should live

so that we're a worthy offering. If we have moments that don't quite measure up—and we all do!—we should repent, making good use of the Penitential Rite of the Mass. We can bring this spirit into our ordinary days by means of a Catholic life of prayer, with its "acts of contrition," examinations of conscience, and especially the Sacrament of Reconciliation, which we should attend often. (Why not once a month?)

As we said in the beginning of these pages: the Mass is what we do. It is what we were baptized for. *It is what we were created for!* It is our only true fulfillment this side of heaven. In the Mass we encounter the glory God wishes to give us in eternity. Then we'll see that glory, because then "we shall see him as he is" (1 John 3:2). Yet even now God possesses all that glory, and even now we receive it in the Mass. We have heaven and we hold it close, though we perceive it only by faith.

The Mass is what we do; and it's what we should always be doing, not only because we go often, but because the Mass, in a very real sense—and through a very real presence—defines our life.

Ours is a life of self-giving, the life of a Christian, the life of Christ.

Go forth, the Mass is ended.
Thanks be to God!

The author, Cardinal Donald Wuerl (*left*), concelebrates Mass
with Pope Benedict XVI at Nationals Park, Washington, D.C.,
in 2008. © *Paul Haring/Catholic News Service*

Notes

Most of the quotations from the ancient Church fathers are adapted from the great collections produced in the nineteenth century: *The Ante-Nicene Fathers,* Alexander Roberts, ed. (Buffalo, N.Y.: Christian Literature, 1885–96); *The Nicene and Post-Nicene Fathers,* Alexander Roberts, James Donaldson, Philip Schaff, and Henry Wace, eds. (Buffalo, N.Y.: Christian Literature, 1886–1900); and *The Apostolic Fathers,* single-volume edition, J. B. Lightfoot, trans. (London: Macmillan, 1891). We have updated the translations to reflect changes in the English language over the last 125 years. When necessary, we referred back to the Latin and Greek originals. For *The Apostolic Tradition,* we relied on the editions of Dom Gregory Dix (London: SPCK, 1937) and Burton Scott Easton (Cambridge: Cambridge University Press, 1934).

11 "an education in Eucharistic faith": The quotations come from the Apostolic Exhortation *Sacramentum Caritatis* (2007), nn. 64–65.

11 the method outlined by Pope Benedict: *Sacramentum Caritatis,* nn. 65.

49 Saint Augustine pointed out: Saint Augustine, *Sermon* 214.

49 In A.D. 107, Saint Ignatius of Antioch wrote: Saint Ignatius of Antioch, *To the Romans* 7.

61 "On the day we call": Saint Justin Martyr, *First Apology* 65–67.

84 The third-century historian Eusebius: Eusebius, *Church History* 5.24.3. He is quoting the second-century bishop Polycrates of Ephesus.

84 Saint Jerome notes: Saint Jerome, Letter 181, to Abundius; see also Saint Epiphanius, *Panarion* 39.2.

96 "a kind of synthesis": Pope Benedict XVI, Homily for Mass on the 150th Anniversary of the Apparitions of the Blessed Virgin Mary at Lourdes, September 14, 2008.

98 "tells how much God loves us": Ibid.

105 "The wise men adored this body": Saint John Chrysostom, *Homilies on First Corinthians* 24.8.

111 "Christ, the Word of God": Origen, *On First Principles,* Preface 1.

114 a Roman governor named Pliny: Pliny the Younger, *Letter* 10.

114 People might forget the homily: Saint Basil the Great, *Homily on Psalm 1.*

114 the Psalms contained "all things human": Saint Athanasius the Great, *Letter to Marcellinus.*

115 "Even if you're tone-deaf": Saint Jerome, *Commentary on Ephesians.*

115 "Are you a craftsman?": Saint John Chrysostom, *Instructions to Catechumens* 2.4.

126 "When the reader has finished": Saint Justin Martyr, *First Apology* 67.

126 "The catechetical . . . aim of the homily": Pope Benedict XVI, *Sacramentum Caritatis,* n. 46.

134 "Then we all rise together": Saint Justin Martyr, *First Apology* 67.

135 "We meet together": Tertullian, *Apology* 39.

135 "to transform the weak": Tertullian, *On Prayer* 29.

138 Saint Hippolytus wrote: Saint Hippolytus, *Apostolic Tradition* 32.

138 "Everyone puts in a small donation": Tertullian, *Apology* 39.

145 the union of the human and divine: Saint Irenaeus of Lyon, *Against Heresies* 4.100.2.

145 a symbol of the communion of Christ: Saint Cyprian of Carthage, *Letter* 62.

146 "There you are": Saint Augustine, *Sermon* 229.

147 Saint Hippolytus includes this dialogue: Saint Hippolytus, *Apostolic Tradition* 4.

147 "The priest, by means of the preface": Saint Cyprian of Carthage, *On the Lord's Prayer* 31.

148 "Follow then towards heaven": Saint Augustine, *Exposition on the Psalms* 91.20. He quotes Saint Matthew's Gospel.

150 Pope Saint Clement of Rome: Saint Clement of Rome, *To the Corinthians* 33.

150 "We recite this confession": Saint Cyril of Jerusalem, *On the Mysteries* 5.6.

150 "Heaven itself may now be walked": Saint Gregory of Nyssa, *On the Baptism of Christ*.

151 "The angels are present": Saint John Chrysostom, *Sermon on the Ascension* 1.

160 "He who stands at the altar": Saint John Chrysostom, *First Homily for the Feast of Pentecost* 4.

171 Christ redeemed mankind: Pope Benedict XVI, *Sacramentum Caritatis*, n. 5.

171 The Church celebrates the Paschal Mystery: Ibid.

171 "The Liturgy is the summit": Second Vatican Council, *Sacrosanctum Concilium*, n. 10.

171 "At every Holy Mass": Pope John Paul II, Homily, Private Mass at the Chapel of the Cenacle, Jerusalem, Thursday, March 23, 2000.

173 "Where there is Christ Jesus": Saint Ignatius of Antioch, *To the Smyrnaens* 8.2.

184 "When I am at Milan": Quoted in Saint Augustine, *Letter to Januarius* 2.3 (Letter 54).

185 "embrace one another": Saint Cyril of Jerusalem, *Mystagogical Lectures* 5.3.

186 "Do you wish to honor": Saint John Chrysostom, *Homilies on St. Matthew* 50.3–4.

192 "The priest says to you": Saint Ambrose of Milan, *On the Sacraments* 4.25.

193 "Then hollow your palm": Saint Cyril of Jerusalem, *Mystagogical Lectures* 5.21–22.

205 "First we have the searching": Joseph Ratzinger, *Feast of Faith* (San Francisco: Ignatius Press, 1986), 47.

For Further Reading

Documents of the Church

All are available online at the websites of the Vatican (www.vatican
.va) and the United States Conference of Catholic Bishops (www
.usccb.org).

Catechism of the Catholic Church (Second Edition). Washington, D.C.:
USCCB, 1997.

Code of Canon Law Annotated. Chicago: Midwest Theological
Forum, 2004. Promulgated by Pope John Paul II in 1983.

Compendium of the Catechism of the Catholic Church. Washington,
D.C.: USCCB, 2006.

Directory on Popular Piety and the Liturgy. Vatican Congregation for
Divine Worship and the Discipline of the Sacraments. December 2001.

Ecclesia de Eucharistia. Pope John Paul II. Encyclical Letter. April 17,
2003.

General Instruction of the Roman Missal (with adaptations for dioceses
in the United States of America). Vatican Congregation for
Divine Worship and the Discipline of the Sacraments. English

translation by International Committee on English in the Liturgy. Published by the United States Conference of Catholic Bishops, 2003.

Lumen Gentium. Dogmatic Constitution on the Church. Second Vatican Council. November 21, 1964.

Redemptionis Sacramentum: On Certain Matters to Be Observed or to Be Avoided Regarding the Most Holy Eucharist. Vatican Congregation for Divine Worship and the Discipline of the Sacraments. March 25, 2004.

Sacramentum Caritatis. Post-Synodal Apostolic Exhortation. Pope Benedict XVI. February 22, 2007.

Sacrosanctum Concilium. Constitution on the Sacred Liturgy. Second Vatican Council (Pope Paul VI). December 4, 1963.

United States Catholic Catechism for Adults. Washington, D.C.: USCCB, 2006.

Books by Cardinal Donald Wuerl

The Catholic Priesthood Today. Chicago: Franciscan Herald Press, 1976.

The Catholic Way: Faith for Living Today. New York: Doubleday, 2001.

The Church and Her Sacraments: Making Christ Visible. Huntington, Ind.: Our Sunday Visitor, 1990.

Fathers of the Church. Boston: St. Paul Editions, 1986.

The Gift of Faith: A Question and Answer Catechism. Coauthor with Father Ronald Lawler and Thomas Comerford Lawler. Huntington, Ind.: Our Sunday Visitor, 2001.

The Teaching of Christ: A Catholic Catechism for Adults. Coeditor with Father Ronald Lawler, Thomas Comerford Lawler, and Father Kris Stubna. Huntington, Ind.: Our Sunday Visitor, 2004.

Books by Mike Aquilina

Fire of God's Love: 120 Reflections on the Eucharist. Ann Arbor: Servant Books, 2009.

The Mass of the Early Christians. Huntington, Ind.: Our Sunday Visitor, 2007.

Praying in the Presence of Our Lord with St. Thomas Aquinas. Huntington, Ind.: Our Sunday Visitor, 2002.

Praying the Psalms with the Early Christians. Coauthor with Christopher Bailey. Ijamsville, Md.: Word Among Us, 2009.

A Pocket Catechism for Kids. Coauthor with Father Kris Stubna. Huntington, Ind.: Our Sunday Visitor, 2001.

What Catholics Believe: A Pocket Catechism. Huntington, Ind.: Our Sunday Visitor, 1999.

Cardinal Donald Wuerl is the sixth Archbishop of Washington, D.C. He has led the Church in Washington since 2006, after serving eighteen years as the Bishop of Pittsburgh. He is especially renowned for his work in Catholic education and faith formation. His books include *The Catholic Way: Faith for Living Today* (Doubleday), *The Teaching of Christ: A Catholic Catechism for Adults* (Our Sunday Visitor), and *The Gift of Faith: A Question and Answer Catechism* (Our Sunday Visitor). Cardinal Wuerl has headed many committees at the United States Conference of Catholic Bishops, including Education, Evangelization, and Catechesis. He is the chair of the Committee on Doctrine and was named by the Congregation for the Doctrine of the Faith as the Vatican's delegate for Anglican parishes in the United States that are seeking unification with the Roman Catholic Church. Cardinal Wuerl is chancellor of the Catholic University of America in Washington, chairman of the board of the Basilica of the National Shrine of the Immaculate Conception, and past chairman of the National Catholic Educational Association and the National Catholic Bioethics Center. A native of Pittsburgh, he received graduate degrees from the Catholic University of America, the Pontifical Gregorian University in Rome, and the Pontifical University of Saint Thomas in Rome (the Angelicum). From the Angelicum he received a doctorate in sacred theology. Ordained to the priesthood in 1966, he was ordained a bishop by Pope John Paul II in 1986, and named a cardinal in 2010 by Pope Benedict XVI.

MIKE AQUILINA is executive vice president of the St. Paul Center for Biblical Theology (SalvationHistory.com). He is the author or editor of more than thirty books on Catholic history, doctrine, and devotion. His titles include *The Mass of the Early Christians* (Our Sunday Visitor), *The Fathers of the Church* (Our Sunday Visitor), *The Grail Code: Quest for the Real Presence* (Loyola Press), *Fire of God's Love: 120 Reflections on the Eucharist* (Servant Books), and *The Mass: 100 Questions, 100 Answers* (Servant Books). Aquilina's books have been translated into many languages, from German and Portuguese to Hungarian and Braille. With theologian Scott Hahn, he has been cohost of eight series that air on the Eternal Word Television Network. With Dr. Hahn, he also leads pilgrimages to Rome and the Holy Land. Aquilina is a frequent guest on Catholic radio, appearing weekly on EWTN's "Sonrise Morning Show" and often on KVSS and Relevant Radio. He is past editor of *New Covenant* magazine and the *Pittsburgh Catholic* newspaper. He blogs about the early Church at FathersOfTheChurch.com. He and his wife, Terri, live near Pittsburgh, Pennsylvania, with their six children, who are the subject of his book *Love in the Little Things: Tales of Family Life* (Servant Books).